Listening to Your Feelings

We all struggle at some point in our lives with feelings so strong that they seem almost overwhelming. How can we face our feelings of anger, fear or jealousy? How can we learn to listen to what our feelings are saying — the important messages they have for us? How can we find wholeness — a healthy balance of mind and emotion?

This book is written to explain the workings of our inner world and help us come to terms with what we find. It recognizes the importance of feelings. It looks at the persona and the shadow and the child within us all. And, where change is desirable, or damage has been done, it suggests how growth and healing are to be found.

MYRA CHAVE-JONES is the author of the bestselling *Coping with Depression*. She is a psychotherapist with long experience in individual therapy. She was founding director of Care and Counsel. Now retired she continues to work in her professional field.

LISTENING TO YOUR FEELINGS

MYRA CHAVE-JONES

A LION PAPERBACK

Oxford · Batavia · Sydney

Copyright © 1989 Myra Chave-Jones

Published by
Lion Publishing plc
Sandy Lane West, Littlemore, Oxford, England
ISBN 0 7459 1210 9
Albatross Books Pty Ltd
PO Box 320, Sutherland, NSW 2232, Australia
ISBN 0 7324 0152 6

First edition 1989

British Library Cataloguing in Publication Data
Chave-Jones, Myra
  Listening to your feelings.
  1. Psychology
  I. Title
  150

  ISBN 0-7459-1210-9

Printed and bound in Great Britain
by Cox & Wyman Ltd, Reading

CONTENTS

Acknowledgments

This little book was first commissioned six years ago. It has been the product of much thought, revision, reluctance and heart searching. I cannot mention by name the multitude of people who have helped to make it and without whom it would have been a dull treatise. Many have given suggestions and encouragement. Others have provided examples and they have all given permission for me to quote them, though they are all in disguise.

The Rev. David Atkinson has very kindly looked through it to make sure that I have not transgressed in my theology, and Mrs Marge Hance has struggled nobly with the typescript. I could not have had a more patient and long-suffering editor than Pat Alexander. My deep thanks to them all.

Introduction

An artist friend heard that I was writing a book and asked me to tell her about it. I did so. 'Oh!' she replied, 'a book on feelings. Very difficult. You are talking about the soul.'

A short time later she produced one of her paintings for me to see. She had done it following the death of a very dear friend and she called it simply 'Bereavement'. It was an abstract painting, with colours that spoke for themselves. The message began at the left side of the canvas with deep, unrelieved, purple. It ended at the right side with soft, quiet, gentle green. The colours in between expressed the slow process of recovery from the depths of grief into quiet peace: there were sudden shafts of orange light, glimpses of pale blue hope, and relapses into dark blue pain. It was one of the truest and most sensitive expositions of bereavement that I have ever seen. The artist was able to give a visual form to inner experiences that words were too clumsy to express. Yet it spoke volumes.

My artist friend has to *paint* her feelings because words could not describe them adequately. As she said, it is very difficult to write a book on feelings. It is like trying to describe the scent of a rose. You can recognize the smell, remember it and explain its existence, but you find it almost impossible to describe it. Feelings have to be experienced. Any attempt to analyze and explain them will fail to capture their intensity. Nevertheless, because our feelings influence us so much, it is important to understand them and explore the potential riches that they can represent.

The difficulty in writing this book was not only that the subject is so hard to pin down. It also re-awakened some of my own feelings that had lain around half-buried for years. That was an unexpected and, in parts, exceedingly painful experience, but one for which I have since become unreservedly grateful. My only regret is that I did not deal with those feelings years ago, because the result has been so liberating.

Most of us agree — at least in theory — that it is important to eat the right foods and take care of our bodies. We also recognise the importance of stimulating our minds with constructive and useful subjects. But the inner world of feelings is often ignored and the many issues that confront it left unresolved.

Much of the time we get on quietly with our lives and are not conscious of strong feelings. Occasionally, however, deep and sometimes irrational feelings may make their presence felt, often without warning. When they rise to the surface of our consciousness, it can be very upsetting.

This book is not primarily a 'how-to' manual on managing feelings. It is more of an attempt to look at some general principles from which we can work out a personal response. We are all uniquely different in our make-up and we all have feelings that express themselves in a hundred different ways. This book is an attempt to make some sense of them. It is addressed to ordinary people who have no particular psychological or religious expertise but who just have to struggle with themselves from time to time.

1

A PERSONAL EXPERIENCE

I wonder what your hobbies are? One of my favourites is 'people watching'. It gives one food for thought, and can be very entertaining. 'There's nowt so queer as folks', as they say. But some years ago the person I had to watch was myself. It happened when I became entangled in an unexpected situation. This is the story, as I recorded it.

For four enjoyable years I have lived next door to Richard and Vanessa. We have not had a great deal of contact. We have chatted inconsequentially over the garden fence from time to time. Richard has lent me the occasional spanner, and has even come round to give me a hand now and then. But otherwise we have not seen much of each other. It has just been good to know that they are there.

Then Richard told me that he wants to change his job. He has applied to a different police force from the one in which he now works, and will be moving many miles away!

I have been afraid that this would happen. Our happy situation has been too good to last! For several months we have waited, and I have tried not to think about their moving — on the basis that if you ignore something you don't like, it may go away. But no!

Today is removal day and, as I write, the furniture is being loaded into the huge van in the road. It is a beautiful April morning, brilliant with sunshine, blossom and the song of the birds.

For the past month I have been vaguely aware of a heaviness of my own spirits but have tried to dismiss it. I have known (and have not wanted to know) that it is connected with Richard and Vanessa's departure. In fact, it is saying goodbye to Richard that concerns me most. I have spoken to myself sternly. After all, we have not lived in each other's pockets and they are not going to the far ends of the earth — so what is all the fuss about? But my lethargy has only increased, I have lost the power of concentration and my spirits have been undeniably sad. I have caught myself giving huge sighs.

So, at last, I have decided to listen to whatever message my feelings are trying to give me. At first there seems to be nothing specific. Of course, I will miss my neighbours very much indeed and I am deeply sorry that they are leaving. I have felt secure and comfortable seeing the light on in their house and hearing Ben, their enormous Rottweiller, clattering in and out of his dog flap.

But the anguish that I have been feeling about their departure has been out of all proportion. I slowly begin to identify this as a sense of desolation, abandonment, insecurity and something like terror. The feelings are very real and almost unbearably painful. They are not made any easier by the knowledge that they are really quite stupid and irrational!

The normal and easy way of shutting out all this unpleasantness would be to work. But I feel too lethargic and I cannot apply my mind. Another escape route would be to socialize — but I do not feel that I am very good company.

I discussed the problem with God in my prayers, and I recalled words from a favourite Psalm that really helped: 'He lifted me out of the slimy pit, out of the mud and mire; he set my feet on a rock and gave me a firm place to stand.' The Psalmist was describing what God had done for him — and 'slimy pit' is a good description of how I am feeling.

A week later, packing began next door. Vanessa and their little daughter Natalie departed. Richard returns in two days time to supervise the actual removal. The curtains have been taken down and the final cake crumbs thrown out for the birds. Everything begins to look empty and has the air of finality. The house, previously such a warm and cosy home, now feels as 'silent as the grave'. I feel terribly alone and bereft. Those words give me the clue I need as I stand forlorn and frightened, facing a sense of irretrievable loss. It is like a bereavement.

As I allow myself to feel the full impact of this pain, instead of trying to block it off, I am carried back in my memory and feelings to my father's graveside. I was then fourteen. The sudden and unforeseen bereavement was a new experience to all the family. The violent rupture of a relationship that I had taken for granted was an unbelievable shock. Father had always been there. That's what he was for: dependable, thoughtful, kind, helpful, trustworthy and generous. And suddenly he was not there any more. My mother was grief-stricken for months. Everyone offered her comfort: a woman tragically widowed, bereft of a man so much loved by everyone. But what do you say to a fourteen-year-old? Anyway, 'children soon get adjusted to these things, don't they? They don't really understand.' The only person I remember relating directly to me as a person was the policeman who had come to break the news to my mother! He had put his hand on my shoulder and said, 'You poor child! I am so sorry!'

So I went back to school and got on with life. I remember my mother saying to me, weeks later 'Why do you never speak about your father?' And I replied 'Because there is nothing to say.' A burial of two sorts had occurred. I buried my feelings when my father went into the grave. Because this was an age when an open display of feelings was not considered acceptable, people thought — as I did myself — that I was behaving with great maturity and self-control.

And now, all these years later, I am confronted with the unresolved grief and pain that I have been carrying around with me all that time!

There have been other significant bereavements since my father's death. I thought I had done all the mourning that it was possible for anyone to do. But I let this new experience speak to me, I know that my grief is primarily for my father. There is a load of unresolved pain. Richard has been a perfect recipient for all that I felt about my father. I felt safe when Richard was around; he was dependable, kind, thoughtful, helpful, trustworthy and generous. Because of this unconscious transfer, my emotional attachment to Richard has become totally out of proportion. (The fact that he is young enough to be my son has nothing to do with it. Neither has the fact that apparently *they* have felt safe and secure in the knowledge that *I* have lived next door!)

So my heart's wisdom has led me to look into the shadow of my feelings. I am still left with the anguish, even though it helps greatly to be able to lay it where it really belongs.

As I continue to face the issue, I begin to be aware, from deep within myself, that my inability to grieve appropriately at the right time was, to a large extent, because I had no one to comfort me. There were people around, but I did not know how to ask, or even think I should ask. I thought the proper thing was to be 'brave'.

That deep wound has been quietly bleeding for years. On the rare occasions when I have spoken about my father I have found myself embarrassingly close to tears. So I have known that there was unfinished business. The time is long overdue to do something radical about the situation.

What am I to do? I have to find some human being who will acknowledge, accept, understand, and be a personal comforter without trying to deny or remove my pain. That will be difficult. For a start it means openly admitting to someone my acute vulnerability. It is so much easier to wear the mask of competence than to be seen to be needy.

Today the dreadful removal day has actually arrived. I have been plying Richard and the furniture removers with coffee and sustenance from time to time. I have told Richard about all my discovery and, although he was astonished, he has been amazingly responsive, understanding and comforting. The fact that I have been able to help him in a practical way seems to have been useful to both of us. We have comforted each other. It has been almost like hearing what my father might have said had he known that he was going to leave his young daughter. It provided an opportunity to grieve together and to find some mutual comfort and 'forgiveness' for the hurt.

In the early afternoon, the great furniture van lumbers off. Richard has cleaned up. I have checked with him that everything inside is ready for the newcomers. He has now gone and we have said goodbye. I waved as his car went up the road, and he waved back all the way.

They have moved. The house is sold and empty. They will not be coming back. I have been given a pretty ornament from their garden as a perpetual reminder, but I may never see them again, in spite of the inevitable mutual invitations. They will go their way, making a new life for themselves with new interests. I shall go my way. This is a parting of the ways.

Later, I begin to hope that I shall see them. Now that I have begun to accept some of the emotions that I had, I am free to visit them with a sense of pleasure and interest, rather than clinging anguish. Life will not be the same, but I am grateful that the worst of the stinging pain has left me. I am very grateful to God for Richard and Vanessa who have helped me to grow a little and begin to get to grips with some unresolved pain and fear.

I am not deluding myself that this is the end of the story. Such deeply entrenched wounds do not heal overnight. Time will tell how radical this change has been, where it may lead and what else needs to be revealed. I must beware of the feeling of euphoria which is really, just at the moment, profound relief. I must continue to pay attention to the vulnerable area and be sure there is no 'infection' lurking there.

But one very strange thing has dawned on me. During all the years, it never once occurred to me that my father might have wanted to say something to me about his departure had it not been so sudden and unpremeditated. I had always imagined that he just vanished, without a care or a backwards look, leaving me in mid air; that he himself had no regrets about leaving his little girl and other members of the family. In reality, that must have been a gross distortion of the facts. In a funny way, the fact that Richard could tell me how sorry he was to leave, and being able to be sad together, seem to comfort me at a deeper level.

Of course, I know that new neighbours will be arriving. I have no interest in them. In fact I almost resent them, in spite of the fact that I have not even seen them. They will change things and I want all traces of Richard, Vanessa, Natalie and Ben to remain as they are. The hasty arrival of a little yellow car, laden with dozens of cardboard boxes, makes me turn away.

Within a day or two, the newcomers install themselves with much noise and commotion. But strangely, I am somewhat readier to accept them. I have had no contact with the newcomers to help me to accept them, but somehow the life of my inner feelings is sorting itself out. I have to start a new relationship. Slowly, my feelings of bereavement and clinging to the past are dissolving of their own accord. Now, a week later, life is reasonably tolerable again and I do not think it will be necessary for me to move house, after all!

As I reflect on all this, I can see other areas of feeling that will help me to change if I am willing to let them speak to me. If I listen to them, they can help me live the present with new understanding from the past.

2

THE IMPORTANCE OF FEELINGS

Taking the time to investigate our feelings is something of a luxury. Fifty years ago, people had to spend most of their time and energy simply doing their daily work. As a result, my own generation was taught to ignore feelings. Indeed, people thought that there was some sort of merit in soldiering on through misfortune. To wallow in feelings was regarded as self-indulgent.

There is some truth in this charge. When we look at the misery of people in poverty-stricken areas of the world, we may feel humbled to see how individuals endure all kinds of pain and misery with helpless resignation. They do not have the resources to meet even basic physical needs, let alone emotional needs.

Nevertheless, the psychological research that has taken place in the last century has clearly demonstrated the importance of emotions and feelings. People do know for a fact that the inner world of emotions affects well-being. We ignore our feelings at our peril.

The most appropriate attitude towards the subject is one that maintains a balance. There are many other important issues in life that rightly demand our attention. At the same time, it is positive and healthy to use the leisure that we have to deal with emotional issues. A useful beginning is to think about how we deal with feelings, and how feelings deal with us.

Lesley had just been relating to me the fact that her husband James had announced his intention of leaving her and their two young children.

'He has found someone who has shown him the real meaning of love, he says.' She wept, and we were silent for a while. After a few minutes she tossed her head and said, 'Oh, I'm sorry. I'm just being emotional.'

It was a reaction that I had heard many times before from people who had been recounting a story full of pain and sadness.

Why should people excuse themselves for displaying a feeling that is quite appropriate to the occasion? Why is the experience of acute distress, joy, or relief written off as 'being emotional'? Why do people trivialize their feelings in this way?

One reason is that a sudden wave of feelings is very disconcerting: it takes us off guard with unexpected strength. It is hard to control and often seems to undermine our self-respect. Even if we do manage to maintain some degree of external composure, more often than not our body will give us some clues about the way we really feel — by a blush, a clenched fist, or a surprise tear.

Another uncomfortable factor is that our feelings are so inconsistent. One day we may be upset by an issue; the next it does not seem to matter. What is even more upsetting is that our feelings sometimes seem to be so irrational. We can cope with something we can understand, but something that seems out of proportion or without cause is baffling. It seems stupid and childish to be overcome in this way, so we try to dismiss the feelings.

Because emotions seem to be able to control us in ways we do not like, we may feel inclined to regard them as enemies. In 1936, during the Spanish Civil War, General Mola led the forces of General Franco against Madrid. He boasted that he was advancing with four columns but that there was a fifth column *inside* the city. This fifth column consisted of other supporters of General Franco who were working in secret to weaken the defences of the city. Feelings can seem like a fifth column inside each one of us, making us weak when we want to be strong. As a result, we often try to struggle against our feelings, to smother them, or to bury them.

Struggling against feelings

Caroline was plagued by horrible feelings of blackness and depression. Her life was quite spoilt by them at intervals. So she consulted a friend who suggested that the best way to tackle the problem was to 'strangle the depression at birth'. She tried to do so, fighting hard not to give in to her feelings, because it seemed to make some sense. But years later, as she looked back, she realized that it had not really made any difference to the underlying unhappiness; it just meant that she stiffened her defences against it.

The struggle against wayward feelings often seems like a head-on confrontation with a determined and wilful child. There is much sweat and tears and the opposition may (or may not) be subdued into a sulky silence. However, no one feels very happy at the end of the encounter. Feelings do not die at the end of a struggle.

Smothering feelings

The traditional 'stiff upper lip' is a good example of the way we smother our feelings. We maintain a strong outer appearance and keep our feelings hidden. There are also several other ways to smother uncomfortable feelings. One is by cramming the day so full with activity or work that there is no opportunity for them to make themselves felt. Another is by deliberately refusing to think about them and consciously smothering them when they do surface. This type of response may be helpful on occasion, but as a way of life it can be self-destructive.

I once knew a group of theological students. The brightest of the bunch had a vivacious personality as well as an astute mind. I was interested to meet his fiancée Jenny and was surprised to find such a serious, plain girl, exceedingly devoted to her Christian faith. Brian was later ordained. He was a good preacher and many people came to hear him and to ask for help with their problems.

Jenny and Brian had been married for six years and had no children when it gradually emerged that he was spending more time than was wise or professionally necessary with a divorcée in the congregation — a sophisticated and charming older woman.

The story is, sadly, all too familiar. Brian had known that he had sexual needs but felt they somehow hindered a 'higher calling', so he just smothered them. He chose a wife who would reinforce this attitude, and he worked hard and long. The more sophisticated woman somehow reawakened his needs. The feelings emerged — quietly at first, but openly later. The mishandled relationship resulted in the breakdown of his marriage, his departure from the Christian ministry, and much confusion and mayhem in the church. Brian did not want to *marry* the other woman: she merely highlighted for him a depth of smothered feeling and somehow 'released' him. How many times this sad tale of misunderstood and mismanaged feelings could be repeated.

Alice was about to be married and her fiancé could

not understand her obvious love for him and yet her fear of sex. The prospect of marriage was alarming to her because some miserable feelings of the past had been awakened. From the age of eight she had been subjected to regular intercourse with her uncle, who had told her that they had a secret together that she must on no account tell anyone. She would not quite have known how to tell anyone else about the relationship and in any case she believed that if a grown-up said something was a secret, it must be. So this uncomfortable state of affairs continued for some years.

Her feelings at the time told her that she was involved in something not quite right and she felt increasingly guilty about it all, but she did not know what to do. In the course of time she moved away, so this activity ceased and the feelings subsided — until she was faced once again with the prospect of sexual intimacy. The powerful, smothered feelings were not dead, but were still smouldering, ready to burst into flames. Alice needed some professional help to understand and begin to deal with them.

Susan had been married for eight years and for most of that time she had been depressed to a greater or lesser degree. She was tired of always feeling 'down'. Her husband had accustomed himself to Susan's dreary moods and the two children hung around, uncertain whether or not they were in the way. Susan tried to join groups and act in a positive way, but depression always won. Things seemed to be going slowly downhill.

There came a time when she decided to try to look at these destructive feelings. She had an overriding sense of having been 'cheated' throughout her life and this feeling was embodied in memories of incidents such as her sister's wedding. On that occasion her mother and sister had been twittering in a general state of ineffective agitation and it had seemed that, if Susan had not taken charge of the situation, the wedding would never have taken place at all! So, although she had been in the middle of her A-levels she had spent a lot of time she could not afford and risked important examination results by helping with the organization. The event was very successful and Susan was glad that she had helped. There was a special benefit for her, too: she had never had a good relationship with her mother — her sister had always been the favourite. But after the wedding Susan felt that she had really earned her way into favour.

Several years later, it was time to plan her own wedding. Mother and sister once again twittered around, so again Susan organized the event. But what really hurt was the comments she received, such as 'I can't think why you are making all this fuss. Why don't you get married at a registry office?' The old feelings of being second-best re-emerged and reinforced the sense she had always had of being cheated. For a variety of reasons she again quietly accepted the situation and smothered her feelings.

But although they had been smothered, the feelings did not die, and they went into marriage with her. Without recognizing clearly what she was doing, she began to demand that her husband should make her his 'favourite child'. He found it hard to meet these barely understood demands and so, unwittingly, reinforced her sense of having been cheated. One result of her smothered feelings was her depression. Another was an inability to recognize what she really wanted in life, in consequence of a lifelong habit of doing what other people wanted in order to earn their 'love'.

It took a long time, and some hard work, for her to get in touch with the successfully smothered anger and resentment. In her family, any such expression would certainly have put her even further out of favour, she felt. This sentiment had been strengthened when she became a Christian. She had supposed that the virtuous thing was to be 'forgiving' — to overlook her hurts and to say nothing about them. It took time for her to recognize that ignoring hurt and forgiving hurt are not the same. Forgiveness means facing up to issues, calling them by their name out in the open, engaging with them, and then giving them a proper burial when they are genuinely dead. That is often more easily said than done. Feelings do not die when they are ignored or smothered.

Burying feelings

Sometimes people split off and bury their painful feelings in a deep dark cavern inside themselves so that they are normally unaware of their existence. Have you ever read a book or seen a play that you have found profoundly disturbing? It may be that the characters or the events make you recall some 'lost' feelings of your own.

Pamela was the elder of two daughters. Her mother was an exceedingly dominant, controlling and demanding woman. The only way to live with her was to acquiesce in everything, which Pamela very quickly learnt to do. The younger daughter was made of different stuff and sparks soon flew in all directions! Predictably, Pamela took on the role of peacekeeper, and throughout her childhood and undergraduate years was known as a good, helpful and amenable person with a first-class brain. Within a few years this 'good' girl was taking on the fragmentary remains of her sister's tumultuous marriage. Pamela was the one who looked after the children and subsidized the family budget. As a result, she had no sort of life of her own and no space to think about marriage for herself.

As the years passed, her parents became more physically dependent. So in addition to her job as a teacher, and her sister's demands, she took care of her parents. At last, at the age of fifty-five, she collapsed under the strain, physically and emotionally. Her body said what her emotions could not — 'enough is enough'. It took time merely to recover her physical strength. Then came the questions about how she could find emotional strength — what she would like for herself in life and how she could express her own inner person. But she did not know.

She did not really want anything except to be able to do her job. She could not cry. She was so far out of touch with herself that she genuinely did not know much about herself. She admitted reluctantly that she sometimes felt cross when people expected so much of her, but she could not say so, nor could she set any limits for herself. She stood like a servant waiting for instructions. Her face looked tense, drawn and unhappy. She claimed that, as a Christian, it was right to devote herself to good works, but the result was scarcely the life abundant that Christ said he came to bring. Something was wrong somewhere.

Pamela had managed much too successfully to bury her natural feelings of resistance, resentment, adventure and curiosity. Had she dared to experience them, they would have produced conflict and disturbance. Therefore she pushed them so far down that she became a virtual robot in appearance and attitude. Not surprisingly, the effort to bring them back was a major task, a long hard struggle accompanied by so much fear, ambivalence and confusion.

Burying feelings in fact causes many disorders. It may be responsible for school phobia in children, agoraphobia in adults, and anorexia nervosa in young girls. Sometimes, the walls of the dark cavern in the inner life actually break down when the pressure inside there becomes too great. This results in neurotic breakdown. All these conditions, and many others, are evidence of buried feelings that do not die. They go on living their own independent life, syphoning off emotional and often physical energy from our external life in order to keep themselves alive. The more successfully we bury them, the less able we are to understand or negotiate with them.

The danger of ignoring feelings

We all need some defences and boundaries. We cannot afford to be utterly without protection from the assaults of our internal and external world. However, when we develop the habit of mishandling our feelings by struggling, smothering or burying them we lose the 'good' ones with the 'bad' ones. There is no sorting device! As we try to avoid the pain of accepting our awkward and troublesome impulses, so we avoid the potential for growth, love, adventure, creativity, reaching out to others and receiving.

When we develop a habit of trying to banish our uncomfortable feelings, we repeat the process with each new set of unpleasant experiences, adding to the pile of submerged explosives. It is not possible to live a life of peace, harmony and purpose at the same time as carrying around a load of potential dynamite!

Social expectations reinforce the tendency to ignore feelings. People develop the idea that progress is a steady climb upwards with an increasing ability to ignore the darker side of the inner emotional life. They think, mistakenly, that 'bad' feelings are too earthy and unrefined to be worthy of serious attention. Nevertheless, the feelings remain within and are a threat to well-being.

Those who are Christians may go through the motions of church-going, prayer, and good works but have no peace in their inner selves. They do not experience the sense of well-being and inner tranquillity that they may speak about or hope for. They live lives of quiet despair, albeit in a Christian context. There is usually a pile of dark emotional baggage lurking about somewhere that still has to be faced.

A balanced view

Although it is unsatisfactory to ignore feelings, it would not be wise to let them dominate either. It is important to understand their limitations in order to handle them constructively. Feelings are really indicators of what is going on in our inner world, the world of our perception, experience and attitudes. These emotions are usually an accurate register of our own personal *internal* reality — that is to say, our fears, hopes, anxieties and expectations. But they may be wildly inaccurate about *external* reality — that is to say, the facts of the case.

We need to regard 'irrational' emotions with a two-sided understanding. They would not be there at all if they were not declaring their own *inner* perceived reality, so they need to be taken seriously. Nevertheless, they may not accurately reflect *outer* reality.

A child, frightened by nasty moving shadows on the bedroom ceiling, is not much reassured by being told there is nothing to worry about. The external truth is that there *is* nothing to worry about and that these shadows are merely caused by the leaves on the tree outside. But the child is convinced that some nameless terror is lurking. If, to take the extreme, the tree were cut down or the child's bedroom changed, the inner inclination to fear would probably latch on to the creaking stairs, or something else. The real task is not to dismiss the inner fear, but to try to build a solid bridge between inner and outer reality without ignoring either: it is done by acknowledging the fear and exploring the reality with the child. We might take the child's hand, show her the tree, talk about it, and stay around until the fear subsides. In this way a child is shown how to build a bridge between inner feelings and outer reality.

Many adults know that there is a gap between their inner feelings and outer reality. Often they are able to comprehend the love of God or of another person on an intellectual level, but it is very hard for them to be truly convinced in a way that can actively nourish and strengthen them. External reality is clear, but internal reality may cast doubts and questions. The person with self-doubts may still be overwhelmed by a sense of worthlessness or repeated experiences of being seriously let-down, belittled or unloved. *It is important to distinguish between outer and inner reality so that the feelings coming from the inner world can be recognized appropriately.*

Tony loved his new wife Ann very much, but she was busy with her job as a full-time teacher and with their social life as well as with her new role as a married woman. She was not able to give Tony the time and attention that he wanted and at times her preoccupation and apparent neglect of him threw him into a descending spiral of gloom, self-doubt and feelings of being unloved and unlovable.

Fortunately, their mutual love enabled them to talk together honestly and openly about this, and he began to realize that his feelings of being unloved originated in his own inner world, not in outer reality. Gradually he began to recognize the feelings for what they were and to distinguish them from the reality of the pressures on Ann. He was then able to reason with himself and make his needs known in an understandable way so that, in turn, Ann felt free to respond.

Inappropriate feelings that are not distinguished from reality can ruin relationships. It is not hard to imagine what might have developed between Tony and Ann had they not dealt with Tony's feelings constructively.

Although feelings are not always an accurate register

of external reality, from a moral point of view they are neutral. It is misleading to use adjectives like 'good' and 'bad'. It would be better to describe them as 'comfortable' or 'uncomfortable'.

We tend naturally to lump emotions together as problematic but this is not always the case. Emotions such as love, joy and excitement can be very pleasurable and make us feel alive, vibrant and energetic. We also tend to think that uncomfortable emotions are undesirable, but that too is not always so. What about the pain of grief over the death of a much-loved husband, wife or friend? It is certainly not wrong to experience the pain when a good relationship is torn, and it is foolish to deny the pain. What about the fears of parents for the adolescent, just beginning to test their wings in a world full of possibilities for good and ill? These fears are often valid, born of experience and knowledge.

Feelings from within are a valuable and important part of our total humanity. Treated with respect and proper care they can become an important base from which to grow to greater maturity. Not only are they important for our own enjoyment and growth. They are also an indispensable medium for understanding and relating to other people. If we are out of touch with our own feelings we shall not truly be able to understand how other people feel. We can put on an act, but we all know it is only skin deep. Feelings are one of the tools we need in order to forge relationships with other people. They are the antennae with which we find our way around.

As we give our feelings room to communicate, and as we learn to listen sensitively to them, we shall discover that they are a living entity. We shall learn to trust and value their wisdom.

3

PERSONA AND SHADOW

During the mid-nineteenth and early twentieth century, many scientists began to break out of the narrow ways of thinking that were common in their day. The work of the Austrian neurologist, Sigmund Freud, and the Swiss psychiatrist, Carl Gustav Jung, is particularly relevant to our subject. They wanted to find out more about the workings of the unconscious mind. According to their theories, the unconscious mind is the part of our being that stores up memories and uses them to govern the way we think and act, but which remains beyond our conscious control. Freud and Jung needed new words to indicate mind and mental activity, to show that they were including the unconscious as well as the conscious life. The words they used were 'psyche' and 'psychic'.

Psychological theories

An explorer who goes to a newly-discovered land will find that a simple outline map of the main seas and continents is helpful. Some parts will need to be changed as they are explored in more detail, but the outline is at least a beginning. A psychological theory is an outline description of how our minds work and can be a useful guide as we begin to explore the frightening feelings and emotional outbursts that we sometimes experience.

Many of us will be very aware of having some inner weakness that constantly lets us down. We may pray about it frequently. We may sometimes weep in despair. It may be to do with drink, sexual habits, money, a jealous attitude, a constant fear of rejection, a sense of inadequacy or inferiority, or anything that makes its presence felt in a disturbing way. Sometimes there is 'victory' at a great cost, and the next time a dispiriting defeat. The weakness cannot be corrected by a simple act of conscious will. It is an example of a problem in our 'psyche'.

Psychic problems force themselves upon us in other ways too. There are illnesses that appear to be purely physical but that cannot be proved to have an organic origin. These conditions are found in a multitude of forms ranging from blindness and paralysis to a host of minor ailments. They may be dismissed as 'nothing but imagination' or 'merely subjective'. They are the 'smoke' that signals a fire in the inner life.

Persona

Small children, left to behave naturally, are aggressive, greedy and sometimes cruel. People who are involved in their upbringing teach them to behave in a way that is socially acceptable. In reality, all that happens is that those unpleasant and disagreeable traits are pushed out of sight. They lurk below the surface in every growing child and in all of us! Given the right conditions they will soon make themselves felt again.

William Golding's best-selling novel, Lord of the Flies, illustrates this. He depicts a group of children shipwrecked on a desert island. The normal restraints of civilized life have gone: honesty, fairness and truth are soon discounted and relationships cease to exist. The children fairly quickly become frightening in their basic destructiveness.

In a normal civilized society a growing child gradually learns to cover up some of his or her raw instincts as well as areas of vulnerability. He begins to wear a mask. He will take it on into adulthood and adjust it according to the need. This mask is like those carried by actors in ancient Greek drama. They had the dual purpose of hiding the actor's real face and indicating to the audience the persona he wishes to portray.

Jung called the masks we wear in everyday life our 'persona'. But whereas the Greek actors put on their masks at will, our 'persona' becomes a part of us which may not be altogether conscious and deliberate. It is an attitude to ourselves and life which has become ingrained.

For instance, a child has to develop a dependable and competent exterior because of the needs of his ailing mother. There is not room for his unsure, fearful self to surface. He soldiers on through life with the same 'persona', so that everyone perceives him as strong, and that is how he sees himself. He does not make allowances for any other needs he may have; neither do other people. Occasional depressive episodes surface when the strain becomes too much, but that is the only clue that there is another part of him.

Shadow

The other part of that person is his shadow; the part where the unresolved fearfulness and unexpressed resentment are lodged.

There was for a short time a cleverly symbolic advertisement for an aftershave lotion called 'Pagan'. The picture represented a suave and sophisticated man whose desirability was increased by Pagan aftershave! This perfect image of the seductive male was his 'persona'. Behind him, almost imperceptibly, fell his dark pagan shadow, complete with horns and spear. The shadow revealed the truth about the man.

Behind every person lies a shadow. It is the dark, primitive, uncontrolled animal part of our psyche that we saw in childhood and thought we had under control. In reality, it has merely been pushed out of sight into our barely conscious psyche. Our social education has not changed it at all and there it lies, sometimes sleeping quietly, sometimes moving about noisily, but certainly not dead.

Jung saw many people who came to him in distress. His conclusion was that it is useless for anyone to ignore the shadow: 'A person's physical and spiritual health depends upon finding a way of living with the shadow side of himself.'

The shadow is the place where we keep buried feelings and where pains and hurts that we were not able to manage at the time they occurred have their home. As children we were too immature to handle even innocent hurts, such as being separated from our mother for too long, and the pain stayed in the shadow. Anything that we do not like about ourselves also goes into the shadow. For instance, we may like to think of ourselves as logical and rational and ignore the imaginative side of ourselves.

We may not like the sound of all this. It seems to be our natural inclination to push unpleasant things away back into the shadow and out of sight. Life seems much more comfortable that way. However, the comfort is easily disturbed when old feelings reawaken.

Mary was unmarried and in her late fifties. She had always lived at home with her parents and now her widowed mother was crippled with arthritis. Mary cared for her with meticulous attention and insisted that this was the right thing to do. After all, her mother had been good to her in the past, the old lady could not help being like this, and there was no one else to look after her anyway. Mary resisted most offers of help made by people who detected her increasing tiredness, and a suggestion that Mary might look for a residential home for her mother, if only on a temporary basis, was rejected out of hand. She explained that she would feel so guilty if she were to let her mother down. As a result, she was unable to make room for her own needs for friendships outside the home or hobbies that she had once enjoyed.

Eventually, Mary's own health began to give way and a social worker was called in to review the situation. Mary was quite unable to see any of the underlying rage, frustration and resentment that had built up in her unconscious life. Had she been aware of these feelings, she might have been able to do her caring with much more genuine love and less of a sense of oppressive duty. Her refusal to look at her own shadow was making the whole situation worse.

The cost of growth

The original split between persona and shadow occurred because it was painful to recall some disturbing facts, events or feelings. The pain, now sheltering in the shadow, pursues its own dark life. In the unconscious, out of sight, it seems to grow in strength so that, when the opportunity comes, it either bursts out in an explosion and overwhelms us or begins to express itself in the form of negative attitudes.

Our daily papers constantly report crime in unexpected quarters and reveal the startling private lives of respectable citizens. Even those with a clean record will probably be aware of the less spectacular offences of irritability and lack of tolerance.

If we are to bring this inner hidden world back into our present awareness, we will have to face the pain barrier which first made us bury it. Here lies the difficulty. We have to work patiently through old hurts, confusions and conflicts. People often want the immediate pain to be relieved. They are not so concerned about thoroughly investigating the cause. But there are no short cuts.

Mary may like to think of herself as a devoted daughter, but the feelings in her shadow demonstrate that her feelings are very mixed. To restore a sense of inner peace, she will need to match her true feelings with her lifestyle.

Reinforcing the split

If for any reason we do not allow our shadow side to surface, we shall simply be making the split between our inner and outer selves worse, causing the persona to become stronger and the shadow to become darker. It is the *split* that is the problem. It is like having a Berlin wall right down the middle of our city. From time to time desperate escapes are made and they cause big trouble. When my neighbours Richard and Vanessa moved my feelings made just such an escape.

Heather demonstrated the split very clearly. She was a popular woman, generous, thoughtful, meticulously clean and tidy, and generally regarded as a 'good' person in the nicest possible way. However, she had always had an intense fear of walking down dark roads and of being in the house alone at night. She tried to avoid difficult situations but, when that was not possible, she suffered agonies of fear behind her locked and barricaded doors. Her fear of being attacked by a 'nasty man' went beyond the bounds of reasonable self-protection and became irrational.

What did that 'nasty man' represent? She had no

idea, beyond the fact that it was some nameless, threatening, overwhelming power that could harm or destroy her. Could it have been the nasty, greedy, mean parts of herself that she was at such pains to push right out of her awareness? Oh no! That was much too painful to contemplate. She despised all those things and could not consider that they might be part of *her*. So Heather continued her pleasant life, in constant fear of this 'nasty man' who lived inside her, on the other side of the great divide.

The internal dialogue

The internal split occurs when there is no common language between reason and the emotions. Healing the split can begin when there is dialogue between the two sides. The persona must acknowledge and respect the shadow and the shadow must acknowledge and respect the persona. Then we can begin to grow.

The paradox

Many of us find it difficult to live with ambiguity. We hold strongly to the idea that things are either right or wrong and anything less clear makes us feel unsafe and confused. In reality, few things in life can be neatly categorized. It is a sign of growth when we can hold the tension between knowing and not knowing, belief and doubt, joy and sorrow, having and waiting, love and hate. But it is easier to run back to neat certainties and tidy doctrines.

Certainly, when we are trying to think about our personal growth, we have to accept the tension between our persona and our shadow side.

A useful analogy is the way we deal with waste disposal. We like to keep ourselves and our homes clean and tidy but in doing so we create all kinds of waste that is smelly and dirty. The problem is solved by having places to store the waste until it can be taken away. When the system is working well, we are not bothered by having waste material. It is only when the system breaks down that waste becomes a problem. Similarly, we need a strategy to enable our tidy persona and untidy shadow to live together.

The potential

Our persona rejects its own shadow. We do not go rummaging around in the dustbin unnecessarily because it is dirty, smelly and contains unpleasant things. For similar reasons, we do not want to face our shadow. But just occasionally, when we are searching desperately for a missing key or lost engagement ring, we may be driven to search through waste in order to salvage something precious. From time to time, among feelings that we find offensive, there is something of value that deserves to be put into a more appropriate place.

For example, the frustration of a father with his layabout son might bear a second look. The father's anger and excessive demands could be masking deep love and yearning which, if examined, could be the beginnings of a new relationship between father and son.

I saw an example of feelings being rescued out of the shadow in the life of Alistair, who is an accountant. He did his job well and at times with enthusiasm, but he felt rebellious, frustrated and angry about life in general. He recognized this attitude and put it down to his inner confusion. One day he had a flash of insight into what caused the confusion. He was invited to attend a party at which the guests had to take a childhood photograph of themselves for identification in a 'Who's Who' display. For this purpose his mother had sent him an old photograph that he had never seen before, and he liked it. Most of his childhood photographs showed a smiling, well-dressed, well-behaved little boy, but this one depicted a non-smiling thug, tousled and unkempt. He suddenly recognized his true self.

'All my life I have been doing things right and fitting into other people's expectations of me,' he said. 'Now I want to be free. I do not want to wear this strait jacket any longer. It does not fit. I want to live a part of my life that has been stifled.'

Until that moment he had tried to keep his proper and acceptable persona well apart from the turbulent and non-conformist self that his parents had disapproved of and that he had pushed into the shadow. The result had been emotional and spiritual ill-health and a sense of inner conflict. He had to integrate the two sides of himself. The unexplored part in the shadow had potential that could enrich his life without destroying the good things. If he were simply to concentrate on the frustration and anger, and try to push it out of his life by discipline, prayer, or some other means, he might miss the potential lying behind it. The potential of the shadow is that it often has within it things which need to be recycled into life again, rather than being totally discarded. It is a matter of not throwing out the baby with the bath water.

Integration

How could he achieve the integration? Remember that his first step was to become aware of feelings of confusion. The second was to recognize the hidden self. The third step was to reflect carefully on the significance of his discovery, either by himself, with some wise and experienced friend or with professional help. (Because he was a Christian he would also bring it all to God in careful and honest consideration.) Then he would find a way to fulfil the newly-recognized needs in an appropriate way. It might involve giving up some commitments in order to make time for a new creative hobby. It might mean becoming more open and vulnerable in relationships. It might involve a new lifestyle altogether. On the other hand, it might involve a radical change in his attitude to himself with no immediate visible change in the outside world. Whatever the choice, healing the split between his shadow and his persona would make him a healthier person in every sense.

However, it would be foolish to throw off all restraint in order to fulfil the urge of his shadow — to embark on some romantic affair, for example, regardless of his domestic commitments. That would leave him no better off than if he decided to reinforce his persona and squash the inner voice. His second state might be worse than the first! To destroy a person's morality does not help because it kills the persona, and in that situation even the shadow makes no sense.

On paper, the steps towards integration sound deceptively simple. In practice it is not usually a painless progression! It is not enough just to *think* about making changes: they really have to be made. It is not just a cerebral adjustment. It is a matter of inner experience which is part of, but more than, our conscious will.

Fifteen years ago Rosemary married a good, kind man for all the wrong reasons: the sense that she would be secure, the idea that it was better to be married than not married, notions of romance and so on. Then, years later, she fell in love with her son's teacher. She felt so fulfilled in this relationship that she thought she had never known what love was before. For several years Rosemary and her lover had a clandestine affair. Both of them wanted to 'do the right thing' and not disturb the two marriages, although her lover's wife was very suspicious and there were many rows.

Eventually the strain became intolerable, so he moved away to another job. They hoped that a small geographical distance might make the relationship more manageable. But Rosemary was plunged into what amounted to the grief of a bereavement. Life had lost its focus and meaning. She did not love her husband and now she felt as though there was nothing left to live for as the years stretched ahead. Her consuming desire was to see her lover again and resume at least some sort of contact. Her distress was intense.

At this point Rosemary was not yet ready to see the whole picture. But if she had had sufficient emotional strength to 'embrace the pain' and stay with it, rather than try to ignore it, or plunge into a frenzy of work or social life, she might possibly have begun to see that there was an element of illusion in the love she received from the other man. She might have begun to look at her own basic insecurity and what emotional needs were being met (or not met) in him. She might have needed to unpack the reasons for being 'satisfied' with a relationship which only went halfway and did not lead to open commitment. She could perhaps have examined the level of non-communication with her husband (of which she complained) and the hidden anger, and to look at the living lie which her life had been thus far.

She had tried, unsuccessfully, to portray the perfect image of the calm, radiant lady who had 'got it all together' and made a 'fantastic marriage' (persona). Now she had the painful chance of calling things by their real names, so that all this dark mess (shadow) might, eventually, produce the reality of what she can be, instead of the fantasy of what she imagined herself to be. Maybe her marriage will never be 'fantastic' and she will have to accept the previously unacceptable fact that she is ordinary rather than special. Marrying the lover was not an option for her. If it had been, and if she had taken that seemingly delightful option, she might have bypassed the harder task of examining the shadow side of herself and her lifestyle. This whole trauma could have been the start of new growth. It would have been hard work and she would have needed help and support. We often have to give up something that seems good in order to find a greater good.

Letting go

If only it were easier to *do* the thing that our rational mind tells us is right and sensible! Of course we know it would be better to let go of something that is making life a misery. Why, then, do we find it so hard to do?

There must be some very strong, emotional tie that reason cannot overcome. We are afraid that if we do try to break the tie, we will be left feeling utterly lost. We cannot bear even the thought of being left like that and so we stay tied to the thing that makes us feel safe, even though it brings us pain.

Someone who is learning to swim finds it very hard to take both feet off the bottom. We know very well that we can't swim with one foot grounded, but we are so afraid of sinking and drowning that it is very hard to lift that foot! Equally we can learn just how a parachute works and watch others jump safely from a plane but still feel terror when the instructor says 'Let go.' *Fear* is a very powerful tie. As we take a closer look at the tie, we also sense that its power over us lies in our great *need* of whatever it is that seems to be so important.

However, there is no way of swimming except by lifting that hesitant foot. There is no way of learning how to do a parachute jump except by doing it! There is *no way* of letting go except by screwing up all our courage, embracing the pain or fear, actually letting go, and trusting that our inner life will still hold us.

There is one strong motive for letting go of something in which we have a heavy investment, and that is the dawning realization that we are backing a loser. The experience, however faltering, that we are not getting good returns on our investment will help us to be more willing to let go.

Uncertainty about where to reinvest all that emotional energy may add to our reluctance to withdraw but the sense of dissatisfaction with the situation marks the first loosening of the powerful tie. At this point our rational thinking may come to our aid, guiding and supporting our emotions.

The sad fact is that, if we hold on indefinitely to thoughts or habits that make us wretched, they will eventually destroy us from within, draining away all our energy and all our joy. There really is no healthy option but to take the risk of change.

The ultimate struggle

One July day in 1941, a prisoner escaped from a work party at the infamous concentration camp at Auschwitz. The camp commander announced that if the prisoner was not found within twenty-four hours, ten out of the 600 men in his cell block would be selected at random and shot. That prisoner was never found: the ten men were selected. One was a family man, a Polish soldier named Gajowniczek. As they were about to be marched off to their death, Father Maximillian Kolbe walked forward. 'I want to take the place of Gajowniczek,' he said.

Thirty years later, Father Kolbe was declared a saint of the Roman Catholic church. During the ceremony the Pope said, 'Millions of beings were sacrificed to the pride of force and the madness of racialism. But in the darkness there glows the figure of Maximillian Kolbe. Over that immense antechamber of death there hovers his divine and imperishable word of life: redeeming love.'

Before Father Kolbe had any idea that this event was to take place, he is recorded to have said, 'The real conflict is the *inner* conflict. Beyond armies of occupation and the hecatombs of extermination camps, there are two irreconcilable enemies in the depth of every soul: good and evil, sin and love. And what use are the victories on the battlefield, if we ourselves are defeated in our innermost personal selves?'

In order to prevent defeat in our innermost personal selves it is vital to achieve some integration between our persona and our shadow. Then we become an authentic person.

4

OUR INNER WORLD

A good friend of mine once said to me, 'I think all this introspection is positively pathological.' He is a fine, sensitive and intelligent man. Was he right? I think that introspection *is* unhealthy if it does not lead to growth and change. If we are only grovelling around in our feelings for selfish pleasure, the activity can become very destructive. But to regard attention to our inner life as unnecessary or undesirable is dangerous and stupid.

Felicity, a gifted and competent woman, was totally disorientated when she found herself alone for a weekend. Her friend had gone away and so had Felicity's husband (for a totally different reason). Because she was left without her usual supports, she felt as though she would disintegrate. She was seized by panic and terror, out of all proportion to the realities of the situation. All she knew was that her feelings of terror seemed very real to her. An unidentified fear was asserting itself in a way that she could not ignore. In order to maintain a normal life, she was going to have to deal with the fear. All she could do at the moment was to run for cover and wait for the weekend to pass. But such irrational fear does not arise for no reason. Felicity needed help to unpack her hidden inner life.

It is unwise to wait until some crisis forces us to evaluate our feelings. Rather, it is worth making an effort to become aware of areas of our inner life that we normally push into the shadow. We may push them away because we do not know how to evaluate or understand them, or simply because we do not think them important. But this is unhelpful. The more out of touch we are with our inner life, the less well integrated we are.

Trillions of biochemical reactions take place constantly on the surface of our skin. We find it hard to pick up any of them except the most acute because our senses are so hardened. It is a sobering thought that we are unaware of many of our emotional reactions. Only an extreme event will bring them to the surface. Then we may say, 'I did not know I was capable of being so angry', or 'Being in love brings out things in me I never knew before.' We can never, in this life, be totally aware of our whole selves, but our purpose now is to identify areas of our inner life that could be more accessible and find ways to get in touch with them. There are several real benefits.

Being in touch

Solomon was a famous king of ancient Israel. He is remembered above all for his wisdom, which was a special gift from God. The collection of wise sayings which makes up the book of Proverbs includes these words: 'Above all else, guard your heart, for it is the well-spring of life.' The 'heart', in Jewish thinking, was the place of the emotions. It was the root place from which the issues of life were dealt with. Solomon knew from bitter experience that he spoke the truth: his own life was spoiled by indulgence, luxury, and lusting after women. His downfall came not because of lack of knowledge but because of an emotional appetite that was beyond his control: failure to look after the well-spring! If only he had been in touch with his own deep motivations, the needs that he was trying to satisfy, the emptiness that he was trying to fill and the basic priorities of the raw, 'uncivilized' part of himself, he might have been able to harness them usefully, rather than allowing them to drag him into a lifestyle that did not bring ultimate satisfaction.

Our inner life has its own dynamism. It does not sleep quietly. It follows its own inclinations and, like a river, twists and turns in and out with relentless persistence until it finds its own level. Now and then it may roar as it tumbles over an obstacle, but it is always seeking its own natural level. Its wisdom is instinctive and accurate in that it is trying to satisfy some experienced need. Presumably Solomon was trying constantly to satisfy his voracious, lustful appetite, but never finding enough and so always moving on to new excitements. Something was driving him with relentless persistence, so that he was prepared to jettison what he knew in his mind to be the way of peace and contentment. For all his wisdom he was not in touch with the driving force from his inner being.

The needs of our inner life are not usually 'wrong'. They are usually basic to our human welfare. There is nothing 'wrong' with sexual satisfaction, the acquisition of money, hard work, pleasure and so on, unless they come to dominate. Sometimes a basic need is so intense that it demands its own satisfaction regardless of anything else. It has become our master rather than our servant. Some of the inner dynamism is out of gear. Anyone who is plagued by alcoholism will understand this very well. The alcoholic is unable to resist a particular inner need in spite of knowing the consequences.

The more we are in touch with our internal life with its needs and yearnings, the more we shall be able to integrate it with our external life. To the extent that the internal and the external work together we shall have a sense of peace and well-being.

The importance of being aware of the dynamics of our inner life is clear: if we are not in touch, the inner life will take over and steer our lives for us, even in the face of our 'better judgment'; if we are in touch, it can become a great ally as we seek to regulate our own destiny.

Decision Making

There is another reason why a sympathetic understanding of our inner world is important: from its hidden position, it can impair our rational judgment and blur our decision making. We see evidence of this all around us. Martin and June had been married for ten years when June announced that she wanted a separation. She no longer found her marriage satisfying and she had been developing a friendship with Paul. She felt more at one with him than with Martin now: Paul was so caring. There were many incidents and complaints that June used to justify her present attitude to Martin, the main one being that he was never there when he was needed. Business commitments or golf always took priority, despite discussions and rows. Gradually this neglect frustrated her to the point where she was no longer prepared to tolerate it.

On a rational level, June was well aware that many young professional men have to spend long hours at work. For her it was particularly irksome emotionally because all her life she had been dogged by deep inner fears of abandonment. She was illegitimate and had been adopted early by parents who received her very warmly and proudly, but whom she felt had never really loved her. They looked after her well and bought her whatever she needed, but she felt that she was regarded as a showpiece for her beauty and intelligence rather than deeply for herself. (This may or may not have been how her parents saw the situation: that is a different matter.)

At the start of her relationship with Martin she had blossomed with the richness of his love, but now he always seemed to have something more important to do and his own needs to meet. June's old hunger for love, which had been kept at bay by Martin's constant attention but never really resolved, began to surface again. Now Paul seemed to offer more promise. Under the surface, June's deep inner need for a constant, loving mother was quietly and persistently trying to find its own level like a river. Now Paul seemed to be that 'mother'.

The relentless pull of the 'river' threatened to impair her rational judgment. She knew only too well from her own unhappy experience that allowing her marriage to break up would hurt her children deeply, but she pushed that issue aside because of the strength of her own inner needs. So her decision-making was blurred by the strong pushes and pulls of her unresolved inner life.

Relationships

There is another reason why it is important to monitor our inner life. If we have a good relationship with our inner self, we are more likely to have a good relationship with others. One of the ways in which we are increasingly able to detect our own inner dynamics is in our relationships with other people. What irritates us? What frightens us? What makes us feel grateful?

Janet was seen by everyone as a competent, well-put-together young woman. She held down a good job and appeared to know where she was going in life. Few people saw the picture she had of herself: a failure who could not meet her own perfectionist ideals, who was unworthy of love, and who had an increasing fear of not being able to cope with life. Many times she would go home at the end of the day and weep with loneliness and frustration until some demand from the outside world meant that she had to pull herself together and put on the competent face again.

She was bewildered about herself and could only say, 'I don't know why I am like this. It all sounds like nonsense, but it is how I feel.' The effort of keeping up appearances was enormous. She often felt exhausted and had minor aches and pains in her body. She even began to contemplate giving up the job that she had so much enjoyed at first. 'What's the matter with me?' she wailed.

That was a good question: and because Janet seriously wanted some resolution of it, she began the difficult and painful journey of exploring her feelings. She began to discover feelings of rejection, anger, fear and guilt, which she had consistently — and to some extent successfully — pushed out of her awareness and buried. She also began to encounter feelings of which she had never even previously been aware: they arose out of experiences that she had had when she was too young to handle the pain. Up to this point Janet's relationship with herself had been very poor and it cast a dark and nameless shadow over almost the whole of her life.

'Other people expect me to be able to do this,' Janet would often say. Or 'other people will think that I am . . .' So she often felt resentful about their demands and yet guilty when she could not meet them. Sometimes it was true that other people did expect things of Janet and did think things about her. People always do. However, the *power* of their expectations or thoughts came from Janet's own expectations about herself. Had the other people not reflected her own feelings about herself, she would have been fairly indifferent to their opinions, or at least free to choose whether or not she would respond. Worse, her resentment of the demands made by her inner self had turned into resentment of other people. She had often been fairly terse and her general level of relationships with other people had been poor.

In Alice Walker's book *The Color Purple*, Miss Celie, the downtrodden and abused wife of Albert, confides to her husband's glamorous and extrovert mistress, Shug Avery, that 'Mister beats me because I ain't you.' When Shug begins to show Miss Celie how to take a pride in herself, then 'Mister' stops beating her.

Another point is that we cannot share with others parts of ourselves that are not available to us. We may be under the impression that we are giving freely, but others will be aware of a point beyond which they cannot go with us. We may offer friendship or help, but there comes a point when we feel impatient and critical. Genuine interest in our friend fades, even though we may have to stay alongside. The trouble is that because we dislike something about ourselves we dislike that same something in other people.

Gavin had coped with various childhood traumas by taking a tight reign on himself, controlling his feelings and doing his best to be in control of his circumstances so that he knew where he was. That way, things and people could not pose a threat of any sort. This made him very competitive in his attitudes. Academically he had to be as good as, or better than, the next person, and his manner was abrasive and confrontational. In his work situations he had to be the boss; otherwise he could be argumentative and uncooperative. In that way he felt that he was a threat to the boss, with power in his own hands rather than being threatened himself. This was his way of life. He was quite unaware of the reason for his behaviour and he did not see himself as being difficult.

He would simply say, 'That's how I am: you either like it or do the other thing.'

It is so easy to find fault with others and be blind to our own shortcomings. Jesus once said: 'Why do you look at the speck of sawdust in your brother's eye and pay no attention to the plank in your own eye? How can you say to your brother, "Let me take the speck out of your eye", when all the time there is a plank in your own eye? You hypocrite, first take the plank out of your own eye, and then you will see clearly to remove the speck from your brother's eye.' One of the reasons why we are so reluctant to attend to our own 'eye' is that it is far more painful than attending to other people's — and Jesus knew it!

We all know people who have splendid views about life, what it is for and how it should be lived, but whose personal relationships are a shambles. This is true of us all to some extent, though it is not pleasant to think of ourselves as hypocrites. When we have not faced our inner feelings we are not able to admit to some of the things that other people see in us. There is a rift between our inner life, with its private thoughts, feelings, opinions and attitudes, and the public life that we would like other people to see. An important test of our wholeness is consistency between what we think and what we say. It is useless simply trying to improve our external image. There has to be a genuine continuity — a oneness between the inner life and the outer life. Hypocrisy arises when we have unmet emotional needs that do not tally with the kind of image we want to project and the things we say we believe.

Physical health

Our body picks up the pains and discomforts of our spirits with amazing accuracy. It is not surprising, really, when we consider that we are made as one, whole, interdependent unit. Our hair, eyes, skin, bowels and almost every other organ reflect the condition of mind and emotions. A well-known general practitioner in an average London-based practice told me that 75 per cent of his patients are suffering from psychosomatic conditions that are caused by emotional factors. Of course, this does not mean that *every* illness is psychosomatic, but it is clear that physical health and emotional health are closely related.

More than that, our body often knows about emotional stress before we become consciously aware of it. What about the man who has a heart attack? He may not have realized that he was under stress at all. Or consider the child who becomes increasingly lethargic for no clear physical reason and is not achieving at school. It is very likely he is quietly worrying about an unhappy situation at home without being consciously aware of it.

In her autobiographical book *Full Circle* Dame Janet Baker describes how, towards the end of her retirement from the operatic stage, she was plagued with toothache in every tooth. The dentist X-rayed her teeth and informed her that for her age (around 50!) they were in excellent condition. 'You are probably grinding your teeth in your sleep. Are you under stress at the moment?' he said. 'Am I under stress?' she thought. She certainly was, but thought she had it all under control. 'I do have it under control,' she writes, 'but my subconscious is peeved by my outer calm and is obviously taking it out on my teeth.' So not only do we have private unruly emotions to manage, we also have a body which betrays the secret.

Another way in which our body monitors our emotional problems is in seeking physical satisfaction to compensate for emotional dissatisfaction. We may eat too much, drink too much, indulge our sexual appetites, work constantly, or even sleep too much to avoid dealing with our emotions. Any of these excesses can also damage our physical health. Maybe this is the reason why some of us have been taught, wrongly, that our body has to be ignored or beaten into subjection and made to do what our 'higher wisdom' dictates. This notion is drawn from the ideas of the ancient Greek philosopher, Plato, who taught that the physical body was unimportant and that only the spirit was significant. For hundreds of years, people have followed this teaching in spite of all the evidence that it is inadequate. There is some point in trying to control the excesses of our bodily appetites, but there is far more point in trying to understand what they are about.

Yvonne had just moved to a new house in a strange area. She had a three-month-old baby, her husband was abroad on business and she herself had had to carry most of the responsibility and anxiety involved in moving house. She began to experience severe back pain and limped about with difficulty, all of which did not help the general domestic situation. The pain drove her to consult a chiropractor, who enquired what had been happening in her life recently. He discovered that all the emotional tension had made certain muscles tighten until the sciatic nerve was trapped, shortening her leg by two inches! She needed to settle into her new home as well as receive physical treatment to get back to her normal, happy state. Even though she was a nurse and had some knowledge of these things, she was still surprised by the way her own body made her aware of the degree of inner tension.

So here we have yet another very important reason for being in touch with and aware of our inner world: the maintenance of good general health. If there is some important imbalance in the dynamics of our inner life, almost inevitably

52

our body will register it in some way that it is beyond our conscious control.

Fulfilment

There may be more reasons why our inner life should be acknowledged and understood, but there is a final one that seems to be of greatest importance: it is the very core of our being. It is from here that we ask huge questions about the meaning of life and love. The most searching question anyone can ask is 'What is the meaning of life?' An elderly person, reviewing a lifetime asks, 'What has it all been about?' These questions are more than just a philosophical exercise: they are central to personal fulfilment. If we are the sort of people who pray and reach out towards spiritual values, it is from our inner life that we do so.

Animals appear to experience a whole range of interesting emotions: pleasure, love, sympathy, fear, anger or disdain. The author C.S. Lewis was a great cat lover. In *Letters to an American Lady* he describes how his cat appeared to sit there thinking, 'I thank God that I am not like other cats, nor even like that dog!' But spiritual issues do not appear to concern our pets! A dog can appreciate an extra big bone or an extra long walk, and a cat may be proud of a new collar, but there it stops. A basic difference between animals and humans seems to be that humans have the capacity for appreciating things on a totally different level.

The main message of the Bible seems to be directed towards our inner life. We are told, and know, that we can have eyes and fail to see, have ears but fail to hear, and be dull in understanding. The clear message is that our physical abilities alone do not tell us all we need to know. The apostle Paul used the quaint and vivid expression 'the eyes of your heart' to describe the type of insight needed to understand spiritual matters such as the great hope, promises and 'incomparably great power' that God makes available to us. When we can truly see, we can begin to incorporate this insight into our whole life and operate with new awareness.

It is vital that we should be open to the riches of understanding in our inner heart and not live our lives like animals looking only for physical satisfaction, food, play, sociability, sport and warmth. John V. Taylor, formerly a Bishop of Winchester, has something to say about this in his book, *A Matter of Life and Death*:

'Every refusal to respond, every evasion of awareness, every choice that deadens, even though it be done in the name of progress or the name of religion is a tiny step towards regression. Which is only another way of saying that the Holy Spirit, who is the Creator Spirit, the Lord and giver of Life, has always been quietly, anonymously at work within every human life, within me, within you, drawing your attention to this, to that, opening your eyes, making you aware, awakening all that is truly human in you, all that is most real. Without fully realizing it, you have often resisted him, finding it too painful to be made fully alive, more comfortable to be a bit insensitive, a bit dead. There have been times when you were stirred with the excitement of a new project, a different interest, an issue of justice that called for support, but it was too much trouble to make room for it. Times, perhaps, when you saw yourself more clearly, knew what you needed to do, but found it too disturbing to pursue. Moments when something strangely beautiful claimed your attention, demanded that you stand and stare, but it was too embarrassing in front of your friends. And when, unexpectedly, God has become more possible, more real, you couldn't let yourself stay with it. These experiences are common to every life, whether they have taken a religious form or not. Thank God that His Spirit is not easily rebuffed, for it is the Spirit of Love. It is the Spirit of Life, striving with our dull, frightened little spirits to bring us fully to life. He has more to give us than the occasional prompting, more than those rare moments of "seeing in a new way". Those hints of a more permanent aliveness to which the Holy Spirit can bring a human being.'

Extroverts and introverts

It is worth pointing out that some types of people are inclined to treat their feelings as important, while others tend to disregard them. Temperament and cultural upbringing both play a part. It is not usually a good thing to try to classify people because there are so many variations, but understanding major patterns may help us to understand ourselves and others better.

The people with an extrovert type of personality seem to derive their energy from the external social environment in mutual exchange and much interaction. They need a public forum to sort out their experience. They need to talk in order to know what they are thinking. They can engage easily with other people and can also intrude on others quite unintentionally. They can neglect the interior life and think that it is not worth examining. They are the sort of people with whom you always know where you stand.

The people with an introvert type of personality, on the other hand, seem to derive their energy from their inner world of ideas and feelings. That, for them, is the most important sphere of activity, where the meaning of things is discovered. They need privacy, space and intimacy, and often appear withdrawn and over-cautious about intruding on another person's space. These people need to think in order to know what they are saying.

It is important to remember that neither of these

types of people is superior or inferior to the other. Both have great strengths and also some weaknesses. Obviously the people who function primarily from their own interior world will find it easier to be in touch with feelings and their significance. Extrovert people will have to exert more of an effort. This in no way reflects on the *importance* of feelings, however.

Men and women

We also have the difference between the way men and women express and handle their feelings — an endlessly fascinating and often frustrating topic!

Generally, a man does not want to analyze his feelings unless something cataclysmic occurs. There seems no point in asking himself why he was angry or hurt if he can get by without doing so. He just uses his common sense to weigh up a situation and decides on a course of action — often irrespective of his own or other people's feelings. It just does not occur to him to consult them. It seems unnecessary, not because he does not love or respect the other people but because it just is not a part of the programme. No malice or unkindness is intended. When a woman complains of being 'emotionally upset' he finds it hard to understand precisely what that means. That state of emotional disequilibrium does not enter into his routine, as a rule. If there is a problem, he will say, you don't get upset about it: you sort it out.

If a man is angry he will express his feelings in a physical way — perhaps get into his car on his own and drive around at high speed, or have a drinking bout, or play loud music, or go about talking or swearing to himself and banging around until he has worked it out of his system. He is most unlikely to have a post mortem about it, unless it affects some piece of work in which he is engaged. Even then he probably will not discuss it at great length unless some suitable person is readily at hand. If no one is available, he can wait, by which time the situation will have lost its urgency.

All this is not to say that men do not experience feelings. Far from it. Generally speaking, the difference lies in the way the feelings are handled. For a man to feel an emotion is one thing and to show it is another. To share it is completely different, because most men like to see themselves as stable, consistent, pragmatic and competent, and a display of feelings makes them feel vulnerable.

For men, there is often a stereotyped gradation of emotion from 'strong' to 'weak'. Anger and aggression are 'strong', for instance, but tenderness, fear, anxiety are 'weak'. To show anger is permissible, but to show fear is not.

On the other hand, a woman's normal reaction to a problem will be to ring up a friend at once or talk to her mother and go over every detail at great length. Emotions are the stuff of life to her and she is quite happy when she is wading knee-deep in them! It is natural to a woman to be in touch with how she *feels* about a relationship.

This difference becomes apparent from the early days of socializing. Generally, boys together will play football or dismantle some machine, but girls will talk. They will talk about their feelings, their boyfriends or the current situation at home. Girls are naturally inclined to think and talk subjectively and our society encourages them. Thus it may happen that many women find their marriage unsatisfying and shallow. They cannot discuss deep feelings with a husband who does not naturally function that way. Mother or sisters live miles away and possibly friends are few, so there is no one with whom to share deep emotional concerns.

Two friends of mine were having a conversation which went like this.

Julie I'm hopeless at my job. I'm sure the boss doesn't like me. I don't think I'm any good.

Bill Well, have you got today's assignments done on time?

Julie Yes.

Bill Were the boss and the others satisfied?

Julie Yes.

Bill Have you got tomorrow's schedule worked out?

Julie Yes.

Bill Well, what's the problem? How can you say you are no good?

Julie You don't understand. I don't want to discuss it any more.

This illustrates beautifully the difference between a man and a woman in approaching feelings; the woman feels them and the man fixes them! Later Bill and Julie had another conversation.

Bill I haven't had a good day. Nothing has gone according to plan.

Julie Oh dear! But I think you're wonderful and I love you.

Bill Thanks! That's nice to know, but it doesn't do much to help.

Thus a man's problems are recognized by him much more easily if they are related to material or cerebral issues and he certainly feels more at ease in trying to work at them in that area. Because relationships are to do with feelings, he is much less sure of his ground. Many a man agrees with Professor Higgins in *Pygmalion* who exclaimed in exasperation, 'Oh, why can't a woman be more like a man?' We know that every person has a masculine and feminine side in their make up, usually weighted more heavily on one side than the other. There are some benefits to be drawn from the fact that in our modern world the great divide is being lessened. Men are being encouraged to develop their feeling abilities, and women's logic is also being valued more. Nevertheless, the good and basic differences do remain; the sexes are different and do express and handle their emotions differently.

Mind and heart

All this talk about feelings may make some people feel slightly sickened. Those who come from a background where feelings are supposed to be kept under, may want to react with the familiar, 'Just pull yourself together' or 'Find something useful to do'. Both are effective ways of running away from the message of feelings and pushing them out of consciousness. The food cupboard is another escape route! Or we may want to return to the safe refuge of cerebral discussion, because that seems rational ground from which to operate. We could discuss for a long time about the various schools of counselling, or even the rights and wrongs of the 'feeling' approach. All that would take the issue away from the actual feeling of the feelings, and *that* is where the real work and value lies.

So what is the place of the brain and the will in our lives? Are they of secondary importance to these great feelings? Of course not! A well-balanced and mature human being has all his or her component parts — the mind, heart, will and body — informing one another and being regarded as of equal value. If any one part — the brain, the body, the feelings or even the spiritual state — has domination over the others, there must inevitably be some eccentricity (off-centredness) and imbalance. Maybe that is why the Bible gives as the first commandment to 'Love the Lord your God with all your heart and with all your soul and with all your mind and with all your strength.' The second was summarized by Jesus Christ (the only historical person who has ever been perfectly integrated with no shadow or great divide) in these words: 'Love your neighbour as yourself', i.e. don't make projections, denials, rationalizations, and so on.

If I reject and am out of touch with myself I shall certainly be out of touch with other people. Nor will I be entirely free to receive or return the love of God.

That takes us round full circle: back to the place where so many of us live — out of touch with vital, valuable, vulnerable parts of ourselves.

It is not safe for anyone to ignore their feelings. As described earlier in this chapter, poor treatment of our inner world is at the root of many unfortunate decisions, twisted relationships, physical ailments and spiritual blindness. It is the sort of condition that T.S. Eliot refers to when he describes people who are 'living and partly living'. But how can we become more vitally in touch with this inner life?

5

WHERE CAN I START?

We have seen that it is important to be aware of and in touch with the inner movements and signs of life of our inner world. In order to do so, we must consciously adopt certain attitudes and, at the same time, be prepared if possible to let down our defences. Knowing what will help and hinder us in our search is therefore very important.

Believing in the value of inner wisdom

The first essential if we want to understand and interpret our inner life is the willingness to believe in its validity. Nothing will ever yield up its secrets to us unless we are committed to its potential value. Any archaeologist or explorer will confirm that painstaking dedication and belief in the likelihood of success is required in order to stick with a project through uncertainty, excitement, disappointment, hope, frustration and inconvenience.

It is just so with exploring our inner life. If we do not really believe that we have any inner *wisdom* or that it is of value, we shall not take much trouble to discover it, and thus our attitude will become a self-fulfilling prophecy. We shall live with an unopened treasure chest because we did not recognize it. Alternatively, we may see it but think of it as Pandora's box: once we open it, the contents will fly all over the place and there will be no hope of ever getting it back into some sort of order. The devil we know is better than the devil we don't know!

We do not have difficulty in recognizing that our physical body has its own peculiar wisdom in keeping us healthy and functioning. We accept that when we have eaten something unsuitable we shall feel sick as our body tries to reject it. We know that when our thumb is sore for no obvious reason, it might be a good idea to see if there is a tiny splinter or thorn. Most of us can trust our bodies to wake up in the morning when we have had enough sleep. We know that our body has a digestive system that will operate without our conscious control. We cannot cause or create these bodily functions by rational thought. We can only help or hinder. In other words, we accept and value the body's wisdom without question.

We are dependent for a satisfactory emotional life on the inner wisdom of our feelings. It is worth believing in this wisdom too.

Listening to the inner voice

From the beginning of this book you will remember that as I anticipated Richard's departure from the house next door I began to be aware of my low spirits, lethargy, sighs and lack of concentration. It would have been easy to ignore or smother these signs, as indeed I tried to initially. But long experience has shown me that this approach is usually unproductive. I am ultimately committed to listening to the messages from within.

Our inner wisdom prompts us in an endless variety of ways, often according to the type of person we are and the sort of experiences we have had. These prompts usually mean that we experience a change in our normal equilibrium.

For Nigel it came in a physical form that eventually became intolerable. He was a poor sleeper and often awoke feeling nauseated and ill. He had occasional migraines and frequent gastric symptoms. He was acutely aware of all this. To outward appearances Nigel was a conscientious, hard-working, upright person, immaculate in appearance and meticulously clean and orderly in his habits. When at last he began to look more attentively at the situation he started to notice that his bizarre dreams often contained situations of frustration, conflict and anger that he could not handle. He began to notice more carefully the events of his life that preceded a migraine. As he put all these things together he gradually became aware that his submerged and generalized anxiety became alive and vivid in his dream life and then spilt over into the following day, causing him to feel ill.

He began slowly to perceive that his perfectionist lifestyle was an attempt to keep control of the wild, messy impulses that he knew from his childhood years to be socially unacceptable. It was extremely hard for him to allow feelings such as anger, greed and indiscipline to come back into his conscious awareness. The fact that he was prepared to befriend these ugly symptoms and explore them allowed him to develop a more satisfactory way of handling them. It was a costly process, and he could only bear a little at a time. Previously, he had resorted to medication and fruitless attempts to 'pull himself together' emotionally.

We can all help ourselves by paying attention to the prompts that reveal discomfort in our inner life. To do so effectively we need to stay with them, allow them to speak to us, ask them questions and think about their significance. This process requires time. We can easily drown our inner voice with the noise of television, or endless chatter, or simply exclude it by allowing other activities to have priority. We must allow it to surface in the quiet times that are available, perhaps walking to the station, washing up, or waiting in a queue. We can listen to our feelings, talk to them, ask them questions, allow them time to respond and go on mulling over this dialogue, trying to understand with 'the eyes of our heart' what they are trying to tell us.

Why this feeling of loneliness that has no rational basis?

Why this anxiety that is out of all proportion to the circumstances?

What am I actually afraid is going to happen?

What would that feel like?

Does this bear any resemblance to previous events in my life?

What does this say about the basis of my security?

We need to allow the questions to take us further and further into the deep roots of the feeling and make time and space to hear what it has to say, just as we would make time to listen to a friend. Then we consider its message. We may not resolve the difficulty all at one go! We cannot have such 'conversations' in a hurry. A relationship, even with oneself, is a living thing and grows at its own pace.

Our inner messages will go on quietly knocking at the door of our awareness, sometimes for years, until we are ready to pay attention and admit them. Change in our external circumstances will often facilitate a change in our inner relationship, so important events such as moving house, starting a job, developing a new friendship or retiring can be important times for looking inwards.

William found this to be true at the time of the birth of his first baby. He looked at his little son and had a strange sense of fear: he felt afraid of this tiny helpless infant and saw him as a rival. That was ridiculous! Here he was, a responsible businessman, who could deal on the stock market with some degree of assurance, assailed by feelings of fear, inadequacy and inner insecurity about his masculinity. It was time to listen to these feelings.

Being honest with ourselves

In this dialogue with feelings we simply have to be honest. If we are to get to the root of the discomfort there is no place for excusing ourselves or for blaming other people. One of the hardest and most unpalatable things we have to do is to stay with the pain of realization and let it speak to us. William did not appreciate being confronted with feelings that were more appropriate to the child in his arms.

It is horrible to have to admit that we are not the fine people we would like to be; for instance, that our competitive spirit may well have its source in envy. But what a change such a revelation could produce, and what relief and improvement in relationships!

Of course, it is natural we should try to defend ourselves against painful feelings. We need defences. However, when they become too thick and heavily fortified they can work against us. A tortoise needs its shell or life would be impossible but if the shell were too thick and heavy the tortoise would not be able to move about at all and life would become impossible for a different reason. Defences serve us best when they are appropriate and flexible.

There are some defences that we all use commonly to ward off the pain of unpleasant emotional insights. Few of them are appropriate.

The defence of denial

Many of us have been brought up to think that feelings are mischievous if not dangerous and need to be kept under. If we feel sudden emotion we consciously try to pull ourselves together. The same stern advice is given to anyone else who seems to be quavering. This approach tries to deny that feelings exist.

Sarah was anxious that she and her husband David should go to see a marriage counsellor because of the difficulties in their relationship. She had a number of complaints: over a period of time, she had not been able to communicate with him; he did not listen to her; he seemed to ignore her when they were together in public; she sensed that he was more attracted by other women; and their sexual relationship was poor, to say the least.

'What absolute nonsense!' David said from the top of his newspaper. 'You are imagining it. There's no problem, except in your mind. You women are all the same. If there is a problem, it's yours, not mine. I can't see anything wrong.'

And that was the end of the conversation. Stalemate again. If David had paused to consider the position, he might have noticed three things at least: he would surely have noticed something unsatisfactory to him in their sex life; he might have seen that if Sarah had a problem then he automatically had one, because hers would brush off on to him somehow or other; and he might have noticed that Sarah's 'wingeing', as he called it, irritated him and he dealt with it by dismissing it rather than by being prepared to examine it; in addition, he might possibly have noticed that this fragment of conversation illustrated precisely what Sarah was talking about! But it was inconvenient and humiliating to do so and he certainly was not prepared to change anything, so he just *denied* the whole problem.

A nurse with many years of experience developed breast cancer. She could not have failed to know what it was and what course it would take, but she steadfastly refused medical help, believing that she would be healed in some mysterious way. She suffered horribly and, in due course, she died, believing almost to the end that healing would come. This might be called faith, but it seems more like the sort of *denial* that David was using to protect himself from unpleasantness.

One of the most glaring forms of denial in our society is the way so many people refuse to think about their own death. Recently I was asked to visit an Over-Sixties club. 'But don't say anything about death or bereavement' my host reminded me. Even in hospitals the death of a patient on the ward is supposed to be hidden from the other patients and is frequently regarded by the medical staff as a defeat. The subsequent empty bed is largely a taboo subject. This is strange in one way, yet very understandable. After all, our own death puts everything on the line: it exposes all that we have lived for, and there is no chance of a corrective re-run. We brought nothing into this world and we can take nothing material out of it. But it might just be easier to *deny* that there is any sort of life after death.

Rationalization

Another device by which people protect themselves from hurt is to substitute a *good* reason for the *real* reason. Maybe someone arranged a party, but did not invite you. You felt slighted and excluded, but to hide your hurt feelings and make them easier to manage you said to yourself, 'Well, I didn't really want to go to their party anyway. They are always boring.' That is rationalization.

Another example is provided by a student named Kate. She was newly pregnant. In her mixture of horror and pleasure she phoned the boyfriend, Mike, who was a fellow student two years younger than she. Mike made suitable noises down the other end of the phone. Three months later she had not heard from him.

'He is very busy doing a vacation job,' said Kate. 'I know he will get in touch with me when it is convenient. It must be quite a shock for him. He is a super guy.'

It would be just too awful to admit that Mike might be running scared and could disappear altogether, that perhaps he was not a super guy after all. She was defending herself against the painful truth by putting what she thought was a good reason in place of what she feared might be the real reason (if she stopped to think about it).

The defence of projection

Long ago in Jewish history, there was a weak, greedy, corrupt and cruel king called Ahab. The prophet Elijah, who must have been quite a formidable character, kept announcing gloomy warnings about famine, war and destruction if Ahab did not mend his ways, because he was causing havoc among the people of God. On one occasion, after a long absence during which Ahab had been trying unsuccessfully to hunt Elijah down in order to silence him for good, Elijah suddenly showed up. Ahab's less-than-friendly greeting was 'Is that you, the troubler of Israel?'

Now, who was it, in actual fact, that was troubling Israel by weakness, greed, corruption and cruelty? Ahab did not like the answer to that question. It was easier for him to transfer all those accusations onto Elijah and hunt them down there. The dark and evil thoughts in his own mind were *projected* onto the screen of Elijah, and Ahab saw them there rather than inside himself.

That incident happened a long time ago, but projection is still a good way of defending ourselves. Have you ever shared in the universal dislike of 'the taxman' who is after our money and who is therefore declared to be greedy, grasping and selfish? This projection helps calm our guilt about wanting all the money we can get!

It is also possible to project good feelings. If we find it embarrassing to accept our own worth, we readily begin to say that anything good is due to the other person.

Relationships sometimes become very complex because we fail to understand what is going on inside ourselves and we project our feelings out onto other people and react to them there. We may say that no one accepts us when in fact we cannot accept our own inner self. Sometimes we also fail to understand what is going on in the inner world of other people and why they make projections onto us which may be unjust or inaccurate.

The defence of regression

Among the repertoire of other devices, some of us use a convenient return to childhood. Rather than accept responsibility for ourselves, we plead diminished responsibility: 'I couldn't help it because I didn't understand,' or 'I'm usually a bit helpless.'

Harold Skimpole, a character in Charles Dickens' *Bleak House* was someone like that. He saw himself as a child, although he had three children, and he demanded that his friend Mr Jarndyce should feed and subsidize him. His demands were charming and unobtrusive, but he held sway over a little empire, as long as Mr Jarndyce was prepared to co-operate. If Mr Jarndyce had withheld some of this support there would have been a terrible outcry. It amounted to blackmail and was very effective in absolving Skimpole of the need to earn his own living and stand on his own feet.

Many of us will have experienced times when things have been going badly for us and we allow ourselves to become petulant and tiresome. We expect people to make allowances for us in our difficult position and we may even take ourselves off to bed, pull the blankets over our head and curl up into a foetal ball in an attempt to go right back to the womb!

Most of us know young children who demand a bottle again, or who have toilet lapses, when the new baby is born. It is hard to begin learning to share.

Philippa's problem was that she felt 'tense and nervous'. She was taking sleeping tablets but did not like the idea of being 'on drugs all her life'. Her husband was working on an oil rig and so he was often away from home for days at a time. She was 'all right' when he was at home but she resented his frequent absences and kept asking him to change his job because she needed him. He refused, saying that they needed the money. When he was absent she became agitated about everything. Had the children got their swimming things and their lunch money? Would she be in time to meet them from school? Would she be able to cope with the bills, her part-time job and the house?

'I've always been the sort of person who needs a lot of love. I want to be cuddled and loved,' she said. 'My little girl always cries when Daddy goes away. That's normal, isn't it? I cry too.'

It seemed as though Philippa felt more like her

daughter's sister than her daughter's mother. She wanted to be excused from adult responsibility by her heavy investment in remaining a child herself. When she saw what she was doing, she had a different sort of dilemma. The old, familiar pattern did work, although it did not work well. Did she really want to change and become more self-confident? Or were the cost and the struggle too great, because there were things she would lose if she changed? 'But I want to become adult *now*,' she said. The need for instant gratification is a sure sign of the part of us that belongs to the child world. In her sex life with her husband, too, she only really liked the cuddling part. 'I do the rest but I don't really enjoy that.'

It was relatively easy for her to comprehend on a theoretical level that she was using *regressive* defences. But we do not change by understanding a theory! She needed to work out these passionate, clinging-child feelings in a relationship with someone who would be able to accept them personally and gradually help her to let go when she was ready, so that she would not feel rejected. Philippa always took upon herself the role of peacemaker and felt personally hurt if she knew that people were 'out of sorts' with each other. She could not tolerate the feeling that everyone was not cosy and warm together, just like little birds in a nest. Part of her was strongly resisting the separateness that is inevitable if there is to be growth.

The defence of displacement

We all know about the employee who dares not kick the boss because of the obvious repercussions and who instead goes home and kicks the cat, or, more probably, shouts at the family. This type of activity is called displacement: we turn our feelings onto a different object. Similarly, I once heard at the funeral of a heroin addict some reference to the fact that 'God took him from us'. That sounded like a real avoidance of an unpleasant truth that the person's own self-destructive habit had caused the death.

The defence of splitting

'Splitting' is a way of keeping someone or something good if it is important to us. We put all the bad things onto someone or something else. For instance, we may miss a colleague who has just left our place of work. We were friends and worked well together. Rather than suffer the pain of our wrath with him for being rotten enough to leave us, we can rationalize ('Well, he was too good for this job anyway') or we can split, by idealizing him and severely criticizing his replacement. All the world's troubles are attributed to a certain group — the other political party, for instance, or whoever happens to offend us most. We each have our own personal list of 'goodies' and 'baddies'. It is strange how *we* usually manage to belong to the good guys! Children used to have their fairy godmothers and wicked witches.

Splitting sometimes happens within a family. One person will seem to carry all that is undesirable and be the 'black sheep' so that the others may seem to be good and acceptable. On close examination, we may detect that this black sheep plays an important role within the family almost as the family dustbin. Most things can be blamed on the victim or attributed to his or her bad behaviour, but there may be all sorts of other things going on quietly within the family which escape attention among the white sheep.

Splitting is easy to see among small children. One child will scream and shout and constantly hit out at a sibling. The child will be duly rebuked and labelled a troublemaker. It may escape attention that the sibling is provoking the first child by quick, nasty, subtle and tantalizing gestures but being careful to avoid behaviour that would lead to punishment. The sibling is cleverly ensuring that all the blame goes elsewhere and so avoids having to face up to feelings of rivalry or jealousy. The dynamics within every family are complex.

The defence of intellectualization

Norman was the second son of strict and undemonstrative parents whose marriage had been one of convenience rather than of love. Both the boys had lived under a burdensome regime of being seen and not heard. They never had meals with their parents and felt as though they were only produced for display to admiring friends and relations. Norman had an enquiring mind and quickly learnt to read. In his loneliness he turned to his books or his private fantasy world where he could make up his own more enjoyable life. As time went by, he found it hard to relate to people, but books needed no such effort: they were his comfort. People represented demands, which he felt unequal to meet, and produced emotions that were uncomfortable. So he developed a lifestyle that focused on intense thinking and reading. Rather than feeling anything, he would turn everything into a cerebral concept and begin to weigh up the advantages and disadvantages. He found *intellectualization* of life so much easier. Many of us use this tactic when dealing with emotive issues.

Subjects such as injustice or terrorism are much easier to deal with on this level. Getting involved can raise dangerous and uncomfortable subjective feelings that are less easy to manage. Similarly, we could talk for a long time about the various schools of counselling or even the rights and wrongs of dealing with feelings. All that would take away from the actual feeling of the feelings!

The defence of compensation

In an attempt to even things up in life, we go over the top in one area to compensate for weakness in another. For example, the youngest member of the family who feels overshadowed and unimportant might be driven by tremendous ambition to get to the top of a chosen profession.

Terry and Marilyn could not have any children. All the possible tests and treatments were done, but they remained infertile, suffering the anguish that only pepleo in that position understand. They then decided to adopt, and used their pain to create a happy home for children who would otherwise have had a very hard time. This was a good and positive way of dealing with their distress.

These are some of the more easily recognizable devices by which we defend ourselves from emotional pain. They were categorized for us initially by Anna Freud (Sigmund's daughter). They are not hard-and-fast compartments, nor are they all-inclusive. It is relatively easy to make lists and categories: we have to remember that they are all about personal discomfort and human feelings. Maybe someone, seeing the name 'Freud', will think, 'Oh yes; we know about him. He was an atheist' or 'He had an obsession about sex, so we don't believe in him and there is no need to take all this seriously.' This could be a good example of 'rationalization'. The good reason may be that 'I find Freud hard to understand' or 'I don't actually know what he did say.' The real reason may be 'I don't want to look at this: it makes me feel uncomfortable. So I shall not look at it and then it will go away.'

Perhaps one of the most important questions in our life is 'How do we handle pain? It's a certain fact that we all experience pain in some form or other. The way we deal with it will, to some extent, determine the sort of people we become. We need some defences against pain and most of us use most of the defences we have just considered at one time or another.

But if our *constant and habitual* lifestyle is to avoid painful feelings by any of these mechanisms, or if they take us over and become a driving force, then we are in danger of losing contact with our inner life. In this way a great divide appears. The persona, heavily defended and wearing the mask of apparent invulnerability, loses touch with the shadow area where the hurt, fear and insecurity are cowering. The persona despises the shadow for its 'weakness' or 'badness' and the shadow cannot speak to the persona because it is hard and unwilling to listen. Thus there is a great divide.

6

WHAT CAN I DO?

If only we could take some action to sort out the problem, life would seem to be much easier. We look around for new resolves of will, new patterns of life — anything we can *do* that will make us feel more in control of the situation. These ploys may succeed in detaching us from the pain but they are often just another way of smothering, or struggling with, the feelings. A more satisfactory, but more painful, way of approaching the situation is to stay with the pain, experience it in all its hurt, let it speak its true message and wait until our inner life is ready to produce its own response.

It is hard to be patient when we are in pain. There is a strong urge to do something that will lessen the pain. But just as our body has its own built-in healing process in response to a physical injury, so has our inner life, if only we can believe in it and give it a chance. We may need help in this process of staying with the pain.

Talking to ourselves

Mercifully, this is not always a sign of madness! This internal dialogue probably goes on all the time at a superficial level. ('Now where did I put that key? Oh yes! I remember . . . in the drawer.') However, when we are engaged in the serious business of trying to cover some of our inner life, we need time to have a leisurely conversation. Hidden feelings do not reveal themselves right away. They need to be assured that they will be respected, valued and given a fair hearing.

As mentioned before, the major changes of life often present us with the opportunity to reflect. Bereavement, retirement, marriage, the birth of a child, a change of house, a serious illness or the 'launching' of the last child are all circumstances that prompt us to ask big questions. The reason is that the enforced change in routine easily leads us to ask why we do what we do. Is it worthwhile? Is there a better way to live?

For example, it is very unpleasant to feel like 'a redundant mother'. 'What am I going to do with myself now? I am so used to being a mother that I don't see myself as anything else — but I just don't want to sit around and wait to be a grandmother.' Questions like these may eventually lead to the start of a new career; the arousal of interests and potential that were quite unthought of before. It may be at some cost, rearrangement and inconvenience to the family, but unless these implications are faced openly the questions may just add to pent-up frustration. The questions may also lead to a reappraisal of the marriage relationship and how it could be enriched.

A man may start to wonder why he is flogging himself to death at work. What is it all for? Does he want to go on doing this until he drops dead?

Asking these questions can lead to the discovery of new potential. Sometimes it is not practical to make major changes, but even small changes can be significant. Other times, new self-awareness will provide the motivation to try something more radical.

The gradual onset of older age with its decreasing physical ability and flexibility, in particular, seems naturally to turn the focus of attention from the outer world of achievement, production and activity, to the inner world of reflection and meditation, and the undiscovered resources which lie there. When we come to an end of escaping from ourselves, of using busyness as a protective barrier, living in a world of hurry, wearing masks and veils of respectability, sociability and capability — then there may be room for unexpected riches, which result from talking to ourselves.

We find an unexpected example of this change of direction in Winston Churchill's book *Painting as a Pastime*. After his political defeat at the end of World War II he suffered an appalling sense of personal rejection. He set about searching for something that would alleviate his depression. He took up painting and began to wander round the galleries of Paris studying other people's works. Writing about this experience later he said, 'Never had I taken an interest in pictures till I tried to paint. I had no preconceived opinions. I just felt, for reasons I could not fathom, that I liked some much more than others. I was astonished that anyone else should, on the most cursory observation of my work, be able to so surely divine a taste which I had never consciously formed.' Churchill used to spend hours in delighted absorption as he developed his new-found talent and way of expressing himself.

Other questions that we can ask in the dialogue are not about our lifestyle but about our innermost selves. What am I afraid of in these emerging emotions? What is the real difficulty for me in this new situation? What do I feel I am lacking? How would I wish things to be different and what does that signify? As we ask the questions, we wait for the responses to emerge. It may take time: days, weeks, or longer. The responses may lead on to another question that will take yet more time. In this way the dialogue takes us further into the hidden layers. The responses may seem uncomfortable, unfamiliar and threatening. We may bombard ourselves with questions and not give ourselves time to listen for answers. Or we may, at once, begin to deal with these responses and feelings in our usual way, perhaps struggling against them, or smothering them. We may need to remind ourselves to listen to the answers.

The small flashes of insight that come to us are just as important as the major ones. An odd comment that we hear or some idea that strikes us may have a useful message. One Sunday morning the sight of a baby lying trustfully in the arms of the vicar at a christening service sparked off all sorts of buried feelings for one woman in the church. She herself had never known her father, never felt the strong support of a man, never experienced herself as having been surrounded by love. She had developed the fiercely independent and capable side of herself in order to survive successfully, but suddenly this little scene broke open for her the suppressed longing and emptiness of her own life.

Would she be able to stay with the pain of that? Would she return quickly to the known and sterile safety of competence? To stay with the scene and gradually learn to trust and value those deep yearnings might help her to be less competitive in life. She might even be able to allow other people to see that she was not always as well put together as she liked to appear. In any case, a level of life of which she had been unaware lay open to her.

Part of the pain of this process is the difficulty of accepting as valid and valuable something that we have conditioned ourselves to regard as inferior. It is really hard work for a person who has developed a very competent exterior and is apparently well in control of everything to begin to value the timid and uncertain parts and all the sensitivity they represent. Sometimes it is hard to recognize that they are there at all.

'You think you are crackers when the adult part of yourself meets the infantile part,' someone said.

To regard the child part as 'infantile' gives a clue to some of the difficulty: that very word has a derogatory ring about it. But the child part has something important to say. The adult and the child have to learn to live together and respect one another's strengths. Just because the child is usually seen as small, that does not mean that it is inferior. Just think how devastatingly honest and discerning your children can be before they have learnt how to wear a mask and before they realize that other people wear them. Think of the wonder and delight on a child's face at some new discovery. Think of the fresh, smooth skin, before the anxieties and cares of life have ploughed their furrows.

Another revealing time is often those first waking moments of the day when we are poised between unconsciousness and consciousness. They can so often speak to us about what our hearts are truly feeling. Are we feeling some vague sense of discomfort? Those first fleeting feelings are full of significance, but they are all too soon lost in the demands and hurly-burly of the day.

There is another way of bringing to the surface parts of our lives which we do not readily recognize. We can *notice* our own reactions: reactions of frustration, feelings of being threatened, emotions of fear and anxiety, fear of competition, and identify the ones that are habitual for us.

Why is it that we withdraw when a conversation reaches a level of personal intimacy?

At what point do we start building walls around ourselves?

What is likely to happen if we do not?

What do we fear?

What would happen if someone actually looked into our eyes? How would we handle that?

What do we think is happening when someone else gets preferential treatment over us?

What techniques do we use for making our needs known?

Can we make a clear and straightforward request without demanding, or is it safer to drop veiled hints? What does that say about the way we see ourselves?

Talking to others

In the normal course of daily life we may encounter friends who, by their kindness and patient consistence, will have a profoundly helpful influence upon us. A marriage relationship can often be a healing experience when we discover that we can be accepted, warts and all. Sometimes people help us to grow spiritually. They stand 'in the place of God' for us, when we can only rise to a vague abstract notion of a God out there somewhere in space. Their care, strength and persistent love is a reflection of him (and comes from him) and we can relate to that until the day comes when we can begin to 'see' God himself more clearly for ourselves and he becomes present to us.

People often look for counselling these days to help them with their troublesome feelings. Counselling is a very imprecise word and can mean many different things. At one end of the spectrum it can be instruction or advice-giving and range through a whole variety of methods as far as psychoanalysis. The various approaches all have something to contribute. The counsellor needs to have the skill of being able to listen in a way that helps the speaker to define a particular problem and distinguish major problems from other, superficial ones. Knowing that our feelings have been heard and respected can help us value and listen to them.

Group support

As well as individual counselling, there is group support. Groups such as Alcoholics Anonymous and Cruse have been of invaluable help and support to thousands of people with a particular type of problem. Many have also found that their church is a therapeutic community, a substitute family, where they are loved and supported through thick and thin and where there is enough trust for them to reveal hidden wounds. They have also found that the church is not a collection of well-behaved and respectable people but of forgiven sinners.

Rob was a regular member of a small group of people who met frequently to care for and support one another. He needed their help now because his girlfriend, Sally, had just told him that she could not continue the friendship. Rob was totally devastated. He had had such high hopes and expectations of the future and found it almost impossible to let go of the rosy dream.

He had had a fairly loveless childhood: well-educated, well-fed and well-clothed by parents who were emotionally distant and whose marriage relationship was a struggle. Eventually they had separated, and he watched all this from the sidelines. Later he went to Africa for a spell, where he stayed with a warm and friendly family and where he blossomed in a new way. The assignment that had taken him there came to a natural end and he returned to England where he felt that he had no home and there was no place where he really belonged. He was lonely and depressed and the group had become important to him.

Then he met Sally who seemed to be the person he had always been looking for. For a while all went well, until Sally could no longer bear the possessive demands that Rob made on her. It was hard for her to withdraw because she knew the effect it would have. When Sally moved out of his life Rob felt as if nothing would ever be the same again.

The group was sympathetic and asked all sorts of questions. At last, Rob was driven to say, 'But it does not help. We just seem to be wallowing in everyone's feelings without healing anything. My own feelings are at sixes and sevens too. All we ever seem to do is just talk about it endlessly! What can I *do*?'

It does help to talk, but it is important to be able to talk with people who know how to walk alongside us in the journey, holding and sustaining us, and enabling a new identity to emerge from the ruins. It is not enough just to get troublesome feelings under control or to feel better about a hurt. Maybe the members of Rob's particular self-help group were not the best people to help him, caring and kind though they obviously were. A group can often be most useful if someone is able to guide it from a position of knowledge and experience, without dominating and supplying ready-made answers.

It is usually a mistake to think that there are easy answers. We are not dealing with a mathematical equation nor a neat set of black and white rules, nor are we looking for a key that will unlock a door. People grow in their own way. Ready-made answers sometimes ignore this personal element. The answer for one person may be quite inappropriate for another. As often as not we know the technical answer anyway: the problem is that we cannot seem to apply it in a way that genuinely resolves the issue or leads us on toward growth and healing.

True and lasting growth comes from inside, not from outside. So it is important to find helpers who have the wisdom and discernment to enable us identify problems and the knowledge of broad general principles that will help us to deal with them. But that is not sufficient in itself. It is essential for there to be a relationship of trust.

Talking to a skilled helper

Jacqueline was in her thirties: she appeared calm, unruffled, pleasant and capable. She was a trained midwife and her hobbies were anything connected with domestic skills and caring. In recent months she had become aware of the fact that she was operating on a very short fuse.

She was doing an additional course of training, which involved living with people of all nationalities in fairly cramped conditions. She found herself feeling very angry if people could not understand her, or if either she or they did silly things. She was also aware that in her midwifery she became irritated with herself if she ever needed help from other staff or did something wrong. She could give endlessly to other people, but she found it very hard to receive and recognized that she needed to be needed in order to feel good.

A few years previously she had had a friendship with Tom that meant a great deal to her. She was deeply hurt when he decided that at forty-five he was too old to marry and suspected he was using this excuse to rationalize his fear of commitment. She had had other men friends but this relationship had been much more significant than any of them.

Her problem was understanding why she got so irrationally angry. In addition to being angry she felt extremely guilty about her anger, which she regarded as an unacceptable weakness. What was she to do?

She began to reflect about herself. She saw herself as a midwife; trained, competent and responsible. 'That tells you about me,' she said. 'Life is about looking after people.'

Then she recalled some of her past life. The eldest of four children, she had had to look after the others, frequently on her own, from her earliest memory. Both parents were working. At school she was teased 'something awful' because she was bigger than the other children and so more was expected of her. She learnt to defend herself by not caring what people said. When she left school she became a nurse and had always enjoyed her work. She particularly liked small babies because they were so completely dependent. Jacqueline began to talk with a skilled helper and over the course of time she was beginning to relax and feel safe in their relationship. The general drift of the conversation went like this.

Helper It seems that you always had to be responsible for other people.

Jacqueline Yes, that's what I think life is about.

Helper What happens to your inner life?

Jacqueline What do you mean?

Helper What happens to your personal thoughts, wishes, and the part of you that is sometimes weak, confused, lonely or hurt?

Jacqueline Oh, I just escape privately and work it out on my own, but the course I am on at the moment does not allow space for that. I can never escape, so the anger just builds up.

Helper What do you think about the weak part that needs to be dealt with in private?

Jacqueline I don't like it. I have always believed that being grown-up was the right thing to be. Fear, incompetence, stupidity, dependence, or doing silly things is something I expect only from *children*. I have always had to be grown up and responsible. That's what was expected.

Helper It seems as though there is a big split somewhere. You have a grown-up, presentable and acceptable side of which you approve and think others will respect, and a painful, confused, childlike side of which you disapprove because it makes mistakes and trips you up from time to time. This child side gets into even deeper trouble because your adult side thinks it ought not to behave like that and it makes you feel guilty. It almost seems as though you are saying that the child side is not part of the real you at all.

Jacqueline Yes, I don't want it to be part of me. It gets in my way, I want to know how to get rid of it.

Helper How does one get rid of a troublesome child? If you banish her upstairs she will either get into more mischief or else she will create such a hullaballoo that she still makes her presence felt. Perhaps a better way to sort her out is to listen to what she wants to say and to befriend her. Do you think you could pay some attention to that needy childlike side of you?

Jacqueline How could I do that?

Helper You might recall some of the things you felt when your own childhood was spent loaded with adult responsibilities, while other children of your age could go out and play. You might think about Tom and why he was so special to you. You said that he cared about you, was kind to you and allowed you to depend on him. It was as though, in some way, he allowed you to express a legitimate part of your unlived childhood. So it was desperately hard for you to accept his withdrawal and to let him go. However, you have now learnt not to care and you have put up your defences once more. You might think about some of the resentful and angry thoughts you had about your parents, your younger brothers and sisters and about Tom that you have never expressed openly and may not even have said privately to yourself.

Jacqueline But that seems very selfish, and anyway it's all in the past and nothing can be done about it.

Helper It does become selfish if you are meeting your own needs to the exclusion of other people's, but actually you cannot really be caring properly for others while your own needs are distracting you as much as they are now. The fact that all these things happened so long ago does not make any difference to your emotional life. There is still something left that has not been resolved. The passage of time does not alter a smothered emotion.

Jacqueline I find this a bit hard to understand. I am not used to thinking about myself like this. But at least it helps my general confusion if I can give some things a name.

Helper The child part of you had to be grown up before its time; it dared not admit weakness in itself for fear of not being able to look after the other young children. Neither can it tolerate weakness in other people. (That is projection at work.) It is going to get anxious, annoyed and impatient when either you or other people do silly things. If the child side of you with all its needs can be accepted and acknowledged, instead of being despised and rejected, it will eventually be able to take its proper place in your inner self. When you feel guilty about your child side you simply push it further out of reach. Certainly it feels troublesome and uncomfortable but that is not the same as being guilty. It has not done anything wrong.

As Jacqueline talked to herself and her helper she was able to listen to what lay behind the irrational anger that was distressing her so much. The anger was only irrational in that it was sometimes too extreme for the circumstances. It was a natural consequence of her inner state. She could begin to trace some of its origins and was thus able to see more clearly. Her helper accepted the frightened little girl, listened to the fears as she relived them, and helped her to face the anger against the parents who had unwittingly placed too heavy burdens on her young shoulders.

As a result of this new atmosphere of acceptance Jacqueline was able to move forward very slowly in her ability to manage her own feelings, to tolerate anger when it was appropriate, and to relate to other people. She needed someone who would allow her child part to be dependent without belittling it, so that she could do some genuine growing emotionally, instead of being stuck. Feelings change their form when we make a place for them and are able to share them with someone who will allow and understand them in an atmosphere of trust.

The process of change

As some of the tangles begin to straighten out there is often confusion. The previous way of looking at things has to alter and this throws our inner self off balance.

James and Judith found this. Judith was an unusually sensitive and perceptive young woman. She said she had been depressed for years. She wept a great deal, lost all her confidence in herself and reached the point of despair. She had had a fairly unhappy childhood involving poor relationships with her parents and she was not doing much better with her husband. He was growing increasingly frustrated by her obvious depression and perpetual tears, so he threw himself even harder into his successful business and his favourite hobby, which was an interest in historic churches. He was very knowledgeable about them and was often asked to go around lecturing on the subject. This opportunity for him to escape meant that meaningful conversation between them had virtually ceased.

One day, a particularly intense outburst with apparently serious talk of suicide made him pay attention. As they had two young children a solution had to be found, for their sakes' alone. James and Judith went to a professional helper. Outwardly, it seemed that Judith was the person with the problem and that James was just going along to give her moral support and demonstrate his interest. As the sessions progressed and Judith sobbed out her distress, James gradually began to comment that he thought his emotional life must be very shallow.

James' main objective in life was to be an achiever. He knew what he wanted and went out and got it. He had never been encouraged as a child to consider his feelings or anyone else's. His father was the same. Both were supremely confident of their own opinions. They would appear to listen to other people's thoughts but they did not pay any real attention. Now that James was beginning to attend to his wife's misery, he could at last see that he was contributing to it.

He was shocked at the revelation. All the strength on which he prided himself suddenly seemed to be turned to weakness and it was then his turn to weep. He was confused about what was strength and what was weakness. He had always despised tears but now he found himself crying. How could weakness be a source of potential strength? How was he to set about understanding something that was so unknown and strange?

James' real strength at this point was his honesty. He was prepared to admit that people in general did not relate to him and that he did not relate to them. He just used them for his own ends, to further his work. He was not afraid of the discomfort of having to admit that he feared being too much like his father. So he had at least two starting-points from which to begin his exploration. He also began to see that while he was going off on his ego-boosting lecture trips, Judith was at home carrying all the discomfort that they could have been sharing between them. He needed to find out what discouraged people from coming voluntarily to talk to him and he needed to identify the ways in which he was imitating his father and decide how he felt about that behaviour.

The tangled network of motivation in the dynamics of a relationship are always complex. James and Judith were reacting to each other's strengths and weaknesses. James appeared to be strong while Judith was weak, but in fact he needed her to be weak because that saved him from having to look at his own areas of weakness. When he was able to do so, Judith could become stronger. They found it hard to make even a gradual change in the balance of their marriage as they both changed position and found new areas of themselves that had previously been submerged. Nevertheless, the discoveries were enriching.

Learning to listen to our feelings is a hard but rewarding task. We have to listen to the childlike side of ourselves that we have always thought of as weak. We therefore have to be gentle and need to listen closely to the actual words that come to mind: they may recall some past event that affected us very deeply.

Remember that usually there are no instant cures

unless a wound is fairly superficial. Time and gentle patience is needed to uncover the layers of pain and the defences that we have built up to shield ourselves from more hurt. Time will also be needed to discover new responses and attitudes and make them part of ourselves.

Above all, we need to know it can be dangerous to walk this pathway alone. The care, trust, strength and support of a wise, dispassionate and discerning helper is essential. One of the tasks of this helper is to ensure that we are not going off on a tangent, or reinforcing some well-trodden path, such as destructive self blame. The choice of a suitable person in whom we can confide is exceedingly important in helping us to be able to grow through the pain.

7

THE CHILD WITHIN

*'I am not concerned with great matters
or with subjects too difficult for me.
Instead I am content and at peace.
As a child lies quietly in its mother's arms
so my heart is quiet within me.
Israel, trust in the Lord now, and forever.'*

PSALM 131, GOOD NEWS BIBLE

Many of us can remember stinging hurts from childhood. We may not remember the precise details of the event accurately but we can recall feelings associated with it. A reminder that 'It wasn't exactly like that . . . ' or 'This happened because . . . ' does not substantially change the feelings. When there is a discrepancy between facts and feelings, it is usually the feelings that carry the day. The emotional wounds from childhood can have a prolonged effect on our lives and cause us to behave in ways that are in some way related to that wound, such as fearing anger or expecting rejection.

The beginnings

However, we bear within us even more unfinished business from childhood than we know. Research shows that from early on in our prenatal life we do react in some primitive way to chemical changes in our environment. A mother's emotional state is recorded by physiological changes that are passed on to the baby in her womb.

One famous researcher, John Bowlby, in his classic book *Child Care and the Growth of Love*, cites evidence to show that 'harmful changes in the environment before birth may cause faults of growth and development exactly like those which have in the past been thought to be due to heredity. This is a finding of great importance which . . . is exactly paralleled in psychology.'

Prior to birth, the foetus, placenta and amniotic fluid were all one whole. But then comes the violent disruption of the actual birth with the severing of all previously familiar physical support systems: there is pushing and pulling, struggling and near suffocation, followed by bright lights, strange loud noises and the new experience of being touched by human hands. Gone is the safe, regular sound of the mother's rhythmic heartbeat, except at feed time. The baby begins an independent existence both physically and emotionally.

Learning to adapt

The tiny infant personality has to find new ways of adapting to the sharp edges and firm contours unknown before. For the first time the baby experiences the pains of physical discomfort, hunger, cold, the strangeness of an alien environment and the fact that needs are not met automatically. Over the course of time, too, the baby has to begin to distinguish between the external and internal worlds. Feelings of frustration and fear begin to arise alongside those of satisfaction and comfort.

The feelings of an infant are total! Any parent can witness the complete bliss after a satisfactory feed or the passionate rage over some unmet need. Such powerful feelings can be frightening, so that a method of adaptation is essential. A silky rag, a furry toy or a thumb to suck are the usual external aids to emotional adaptation. This process continues over the early months and years while the child is struggling with the lack of 'fit' between the self and the environment.

The adults whose task it is to care for the child also have to adapt. They must struggle to understand, as best they can, the primitive and rudimentary language of cries, restlessness, sleep and physical communication. This is no easy task, especially for the inexperienced. Even the best parents fail, from time to time, leaving the child with some kind of pain. The baby will soon begin to know whether or not effective comfort will usually come from outside. If it does, the child can begin to send out tiny roots of trust; when it does not, the child has to turn inward to his own inadequate resources to defend himself against the pain.

A small child is vulnerable because of extreme dependence. If the external environment is too unsympathetic this child may not be able to make a very good adjustment to its demands. The baby will not carry all this into conscious awareness: the pains and struggle will be buried deeply. In an emotional sense, as the child grows he will be living above a 'geological fault' as a result of which he will experience periodic tremors and earthquakes. It is a buried trauma but it will affect the way he responds to subsequent pressure. Further emotional development will be influenced by the comfort the child receives from his chosen method of adaptation and by the quality of care the parents provide.

A healthy, caring relationship is established slowly and sensitively. Within the intimacy and closeness of the feeding situation the symbiotic union of prenatal life is temporarily restored. These frequent returns help the baby to manage life in between times.

The growth of trust

The parents learn to recognize other physical and emotional needs of the infant, and they begin to learn one another's language. Over the period of the early years, but especially in the early months, through the repeated experience of needs being met, promises being kept, boundaries being maintained and limitations being accepted, the caring parents establish a relationship of which *trust* is the basic ingredient.

Initially it is a physical relationship: feeding, holding, cleaning, gazing and so on. The infant demonstrates trust by taking food and digesting it easily and by sleeping well.

Parents cannot always be present, and even if they could, there are some pains that they cannot relieve: but the child learns that where there is pain there is also comfort and that all will become well. Parents can comfort because they know what pain feels like: they have had bad toothache, or tummy-ache, or have been furious or hungry. A parent can contain the painful feelings of the baby and know when to intervene and when not to. The baby can be in the same room and allowed to be alone, thus developing the child's trustful capacity to be in harmony whilst separate, learning to trust in silence, when nothing is happening — no physical excitement, no talk, no activity and no distractions which can cover up fears of loneliness and thus put the baby out of touch with him or herself. In this way the child's external world of physical senses and inner world of emotions and feelings develop alongside one another.

It is the *repeated* experience of consistency and continuity that builds up confidence, trust and love. The child is gradually able to let the parent out of sight without feeling undue anxiety or rage. The sense of developing trust makes it possible to adjust to the postnatal environment, to rely on the consistency of the outer world and to feel that the violent urges and needs of the inner world are therefore manageable.

All relationships consist of the ebb and flow of communication, action and reaction. The infant offers trust in response to the quality of care. In turn this trust leads to love and a warm, responsive exchange between parent and child. Trust and love can only develop within a relationship. We develop the capacity to love because someone first loved us.

I was in a shop one day buying some toothpaste. The sound of half-choked sobs made me look round and I saw a small girl, aged about three, trailing miserably after her cross-looking mother who was pushing a young baby in a buggy. The toddler was clutching some object, which the mother snatched from her, paid for and shoved back into her hand. She then stalked out of the shop at an angry adult's pace. At the check-out the toddler's sobs subsided. The small girl literally choked them back inside herself, received the object with no pleasure and straggled after her mother in utter dejection. She had no alternative but to follow her mother because she was too young to be independent. What could she do with her feelings of hurt, fear, disappointment, rage, except to swallow them out of sight? I wondered what she had done with all the feelings that she must have experienced when the new baby was born and she had to give up her place in the buggy, walk like a big girl and share her mother.

On this occasion there was apparently no one to understand and help her to hold the love, the misery and the confusion together with responding love and patience. My own little smile of encouragement went unheeded. I was an unknown stranger with whom she had no relationship and of whom she had no expectations. The next thing this little girl might get for straggling behind was a shout or a slap, which would actually make her feel even more alone and unhappy. Children often have their emotional desires and needs frustrated and they suffer all the terror of being angry with the parent whom they love and on whom they depend utterly. So the great divide begins to appear.

Self-worth and confidence

In the healthy developing inner self, there will be a strong sense of self-worth that comes from the nurturing experiences of trust and love. This sense of worth carries with it a sense of being confident about who one is and the acceptability of what one can do, as well as a proper regard of others.

This self-confidence (in the proper sense of the word) will leave the individual room for questioning, doubts and change about beliefs, values and customs; it will allow freedom to explore new places, ideas, situations and relationships; it will allow for play, experimentation and discovery; it will make risk-taking a possibility; it will permit both physical and emotional intimacy and also be able to tolerate separateness; it will not demand instant gratification; it will allow the individual to trust, understand and have pleasure in his or her own emotions and physical sensations; above all and because this self-confidence has been born of trust in someone else, it will allow the individual to express anger, without which love can be inhibited.

This is a picture of maturity that most of us would envy! It is a rare person whose inner life and outer life are well integrated, who has no great internal divide that gets in the way of enjoying life in all its fullness. It is as a result of early disappointments when the significant caregiver failed to meet our needs that we develop the false persona to deal with the outside world and a shadow in which to hide our true feelings.

The growth of trust in God

I believe that our basic capacity to trust in God is conditioned by our early experiences. If our parents provide us with the type of care that makes us feel that we can trust them to love us consistently and be confident that they will help soothe our pain, then we have the sort of foundational experience that will later allow us to trust in God. If our parents have made our childhood world one in which good experiences outnumber bad ones then our experience will help us to believe in God. We will evaluate the painful and difficult experiences of our inner and outer life as well as the satisfying and pleasurable ones and discover that, on balance, the good outweighs the bad and that there is indeed a God who loves us and cares for us.

Objective, academic doctrine by itself will not enable a person to do this. The intellectual knowledge that parents are there to protect and care for their child will not help me when I have painful teeth coming through or have fallen down and cut my knee. It is the gentle care and soothing ointments from parents who themselves have experienced pain that will help me, although it will not take the pain away altogether. This experience of God being with us in both the pain and also the comfort is summed up in the shepherd imagery of Psalm 23: 'Even though I walk through the valley of the shadow of death

I will fear no evil, for you are with me; your rod and staff they comfort me.'

The important phrase is 'for you are with me'. All troubles are much worse if we feel abandoned and isolated. In the human situation most parents are sufficiently committed to their children to stay with them by night and day if necessary and not leave them floundering and afraid. The love and commitment of human parents is a reflection of a greater commitment by an almighty God and a demonstration that at the end of the day, all will be well.

The growth of trust in self

In addition to trust in God, there will also emerge a trust in ourselves, a genuine belief in our own worth based not on endeavours but on the gift of being cherished. This confidence is valuable in its own right. It is also valuable because it makes it easier for us to accept the Christian teaching that we are acceptable to God because he is loving and merciful and not because we have done good things.

This is the great initial discovery that the reformer Martin Luther made and that transformed him from being a trembling, guilt-ridden monk, afraid to officiate at the Mass, to a free man. That discovery was progressive and gradually affected other areas of his life.

By contrast, the child whose parents were frightening, over-indulgent, unreliable or simply not there, may have to wrestle with periods of self-doubt, depression and black feelings of dereliction from time to time as life goes on. Since no one has had a perfect parenting situation, everyone has residual needs that interfere with smooth relationships with both God and our fellow human beings. *We all have the remains of the crying, needy baby inside ourselves, no matter how grown up we are.* The way to growth and maturity is not the elimination of the child, as mentioned earlier, but integration of the adult side with the child side of ourselves.

Sins or needs

We all behave, at times, in ways that are destructive to ourselves and others. Our actions may be disappointing, futile or worse. This behaviour results from an internal unhappiness, from the disease of sin with which we were infected by virtue of having been born into a 'fallen' world — a factor which most of us recognize if we allow ourselves to reflect on it.

As we think further, we realize that some of our behaviour comes from deliberate occasions of sheer cussedness, awkwardness or selfishness. We do not have to give vent to the inner nastiness in this way, and we do not always. But just sometimes we let it out because that satisfies us, in a miserable sort of way!

However, there are other times when we seem to be taken over by an all-consuming drive that is quite beyond our control. We know that a certain reaction or line of behaviour is in no one's best interests but we just cannot help following that overwhelming inner urge. It may be compulsive jealousy, lying, the desire for drink, sex, drugs, gambling or stealing, or other immediate relief for the terrible hunger within. We seem powerless. This pressure can often be traced back to intensely painful experiences in childhood when the emerging personality was unable to bear the intensity of broken trust and love withdrawn.

Learning to trust again is a slow business. Falling in love can happen at the drop of a hat, but learning to love has to be hammered out through thick and thin. So has trust.

There is no clear-cut line between sin and need; they merge and intertwine and are both evidence that we live in a damaged and imperfect world. It is often a long work of grace by the Holy Spirit of God, usually in conjunction with human helpers, to heal some of these injuries and meet the needs. The individual is not responsible for the fact that damage has been inflicted, but is nevertheless responsible for seeking to change and grow. It is not acceptable to sit back and blame the environment or our parents. Both deliberate and compulsive destructiveness are included in the prayer for forgiveness in the *Book of Common Prayer*. It acknowledges to God that 'we have sinned against You and against our fellow men in thought, word and deed, through ignorance, through weakness, through our own deliberate fault'. Some behaviour — such as consistent inability to control ourselves, compulsive jealousy or sexual difficulties — is likely to be a 'sin' of weakness.

The invitation we sometimes hear to 'put your trust in God' may be fairly meaningless to those of us whose capacity for trust has been seriously damaged, although we may be longing to believe that there is a trustworthy being somewhere. Proof of trustworthiness and the ability to trust are inextricably interwoven, however, and disappointments with people can make us unwilling to risk trusting God. Then again, the shallow presentation of a God who is a panacea for all earthly ills leads to disillusionment.

God is indeed caring and can hold together both the pain and the comfort at the same time. It seems that a personal turning to God, like healing, is usually a gradual process, though it may manifest itself suddenly. It is an ongoing process into maturity of relationship with God and an outworking into the spiritual, social, physical and emotional areas of life.

This ongoing process of trust includes the growing

ability to face and accept the formerly rejected and despised parts of ourselves that are exercising a destructive force in the inner life. These are the feelings that have been buried so deeply that we are unaware of them as well as feelings that are repressed or inhibited by conscious control. In the atmosphere of love and trust, it will become increasingly possible to reach those fearsome depths that, because of their very pain and rage, have been pushed into inaccessible regions. Although the feelings — such as jealousy, meanness, greed, hatred, fear, dishonesty and conceit — present themselves as unacceptable, it will become possible to admit that they are actually part of us instead of blaming someone else or using one of the other well-known defence mechanisms.

As the needy, meaningless, vulnerable person is gradually called from the dark cellars into warm, loving acceptance, the destructive energies of all those painful feelings are slowly transformed into creative life. They are not totally a mess to be cleared up but rather a strength to be rechannelled. We could say that they represent some of the contents of the dustbin to be recycled as we gradually become new people. The basic feelings themselves are not bad; they have simply become twisted with pain and distorted by attempts to defend themselves from that pain. As a result, they appear very unattractive.

We are fully accepted by God, who has long known about those buried and smothered parts that we have tried to banish. Therefore we can begin to accept ourselves. When this deep realization is based on personal experience and not just theory, we are brought to the point of conversion. The experience seems to have some similarity with the New Testament story of the tax-gatherer who recognized the many conflicting aspects of himself and had enough trust to be able to admit it in his prayer. 'God have mercy on me, a sinner.' This man, Luke's Gospel records, went home 'in a right relationship with God'. The self-righteous Pharisee, who was in the temple praying at the same time, remained content in his split-off complacency, projecting his own faults onto the other man, and condemning it there instead of in himself. 'I thank God I am not like other men.'

The story of the Prodigal Son as told by Luke is a similar contrast of two people. The one son was able to accept the wretchedness that caused such pain to himself and to his father; the other preferred the dubious comfort of self-righteousness, because the humiliation of facing the split-off bits of himself (as reflected in his brother) were too uncomfortable.

Both the self-righteous persons in these two stories ended with a poor relationship because they could not face their shadow selves. The ones who were able to acknowledge the rotten things within them were the ones who were able to have a relationship with God.

Help from beyond ourselves

We often find that we are indebted to some flesh-and-blood person who helps us change in a positive way. I call this process 'incarnational intervention'. People cannot be born, grow or change in a vacuum. *We can only live within relationships*. The Bible is about our relationship with God through Jesus and then about our relationships with one another and ourselves. The first casualty of free will was our relationship with God, and the constant message of God to his people all down the ages has been that he was offering a restored relationship. But it was too demanding a message for people to hear: it involved facing the truth about themselves.

So finally God came himself and became a human

being in the person of Jesus Christ, as an historic person. As he walked about the streets and in the fields of Palestine, he taught and worked miracles based on the same principles: people who wanted to be healed had to face what was wrong and admit it honestly, so that they could be in a position to accept healing of the body and of the inner life and relationships. Jesus was not simply interested in pain relief, which so many people would have preferred then, as they still do today. There had to be radical honesty.

But Jesus Christ did not just dispense cheap healing at no personal cost. He also experienced the pangs of being misunderstood and betrayed by those who were close to him, and treated unjustly by the people who had power. He accepted all the insane projections of anger of the self-righteous people. As the prophet Isaiah had foretold, 'he bore our griefs and carried our sorrows' and in his own physical body he allowed himself to be rejected. He was tortured and done to death like a common criminal for offences in which he did not take part: for our sins, our griefs, our pains and stupidities, and the anguish of a world distorted from the original plan of its creator.

So although he was deeply involved in all our 'mess' he was not part of it. In some way which is beyond our comprehension, we can 'see' that God came alongside our distress and helplessness in the most intimate way possible. His 'incarnational intervention' — by taking on himself the ultimate result, in death, of all our wayward destructiveness — and his subsequent resurrection, makes it possible for us to enjoy a restored relationship with God. In this new relationship we can face all the aspects of our distorted nature and the fear which such an encounter brings. He himself can hold, comfort and heal our pain because he knows the pain of broken relationships by identification with us. We can continue to deepen that relationship in verbal, meditative and contemplative prayer as we proceed along life's journey. Love and trust are the essential requisites.

Human helpers

The need for human beings to help one another in their distress has existed since the world began. For the ancient Greeks and Romans the philosopher was the 'healer of the soul'. The Roman philosopher Cicero, who lived a few years before Christ, said that 'the soul that is sick cannot rightly prescribe for itself except by following the instruction of wise men.' During the early centuries AD, the church took the main responsibility for the cure and care of soul, in which Jesus Christ had a unique place in providing a remedy for sin and in assisting spiritual growth. Probably professional psychotherapy began to take over from religion in an effort to fill the spiritual void left by the decline in religious belief. But the principles are the same. The deep buried pains of the initial relationship can be experienced again and healed through this new professional relationship which is based on love and trust. Discussing things in intellectual terms and reading helpful books can be of limited use, but they cannot possibly reach the sore places with the loving touch of healing that can be experienced within a living relationship. The healing comes not by talking about feelings but by actually experiencing them within this safe context. The adaptive defences that have been erected so carefully and so firmly to protect us from pain will be gently exposed and slowly rendered unnecessary.

This time the great difference is that there is someone alongside who can feel the pain, even if that person cannot take it away. This someone shares in the pain with us so that the fears and hates and buried needs of the child within, previously ignored, can now be understood, acknowledged and integrated with the loving feelings and be held together. It is the sharing which is important.

This process is costly to the therapist, who must suffer with the patient to a large degree and pick up part of the pain through personal identification with the patient. But at the same time, the therapist does not become totally immersed in the mess. On a limited level, this is a reflection of God's intervention.

Thus far psychotherapy is consistent with Christian faith, in its concern with growth and wholeness, with attitudes, feelings and behaviour. Both have theories about the nature of human beings and the causes of behaviour. Both acknowledge the importance of recognizing the dark side of ourselves, not so that we can act on those feelings, but because if we suppress them they are then able to exert an influence that is unpredictable and may be uncontrollable. Psychotherapy does not lay down rules about how we should behave in specific circumstances, but rather tries to help us to realize our full potential from our inner resources.

There are divergences between the Christian faith and some forms of psychotherapy, however. The Christian faith, while encouraging us to realize our potential, offers us something beyond ourselves. The objective and external God is present in the universe as well as within us and he offers a restored relationship with him and his grace to help us to grow. Sadly, of course, the Christian faith has been misunderstood simply as a sort of moral code with rules that must be kept. Because owning up to bad feelings would represent breaking that code, people work even harder to push such feelings underground where they become inaccessible. The truth is that Christianity rests upon the foundation of a relationship of costly love that brings inner healing in a restored relationship with God.

8

SOME SPECIFIC EMOTIONS

The influence of the very early years is absolutely crucial to our subsequent development. Our helplessness as children makes us a prey to all the strength of deep emotional needs for love, warmth and trust that are essential to our survival. The tender seedling cannot bear the harsh night frosts of neglect, and our infant selves cannot bear misunderstanding or too little love. As children we lack the verbal skills to express our needs and the experience to act as a balance to the intensity of the immediate present. Our feelings of rage or delight are total and can swing quickly from one extreme to the other. We have no internal moderator of our needs and can only acquire one slowly and gradually as we learn to trust that, on the whole, someone does care and that our needs will be met within the limited time that we can wait.

The child who is adequately cared for will radiate physical and emotional satisfaction. There are few more moving experiences than to look into the open face of a child who has not yet had to learn too deeply about suffering and defences and to see the excitement, the trust and the reaching out into life.

Guilt and the sense of rejection

If, as time passes, we sense criticism and rejection because we do not come up to our parents' expectations, or if too heavy emotional burdens are put upon our small shoulders, we will take into ourselves a sense of disapproval and inadequacy. If we are not loved and valued by our parents, how can we love and value ourselves? And if we cannot love and value ourselves how can we relate warmly to other people with any genuine depth of love? Our 'love' will always have attached to it the craving for approval, which in turn produces anxiety.

This sense of low self-esteem will produce an over-all sense of *guilt*. It is not that we have, in fact, done anything wrong, but there is a pervasive atmosphere of not having made the grade. It is not real guilt, but a generalized feeling of dis-ease which makes us feel that we must placate people all the time and apologize for ourselves constantly. We are never sure when we have done enough to earn approval. We become the sort of person who needs to be needed and will spend our lives taking care of people and being good in order to confirm that we are acceptable. Left on our own, we are assailed by terrible doubts about ourselves and our value.

This is a highly unsatisfactory way to live. The need for approval means that we can never be ourselves. We must always try to fit the image of what we would like people to think about us. If we should ever want to cast off that straitjacket we feel greatly anxious about the danger of losing people's 'love'.

Relationships based on the need to be needed are always a trap. They are not based on love and trust and are therefore conditional. 'Oh, but everyone needs to be needed,' people say, 'it's natural.' Not so. If being needed and indispensable to other people is the way in which we receive our sense of inner affirmation and worth, we are in bondage. However, if we choose from time to time to put ourselves in the position of being needed and can then emerge again freely, that is a different matter.

If we are plagued by false guilt we will usually find it difficult to forgive ourselves. Despite all external reassurances of acceptance, love and forgiveness, we will go on feeling bad inside. It seems irrational, and we know it, but that is how it is.

As soon as we hear the word 'irrational' we should begin to look below the surface for reasons in the inner life. More than likely, we shall encounter the child within us who is bearing all the marks of low self-esteem. We cannot accept ourselves because as children we did not feel accepted at gut level; verbal reassurance is ineffectual now. We will be projecting outward onto other people our own inner sense of condemnation: 'I think I am bad, so they must think I am bad.'

If we are aware of God, it is likely that we will picture a legalistic tyrant, a sadistic monster who is obsessed with all the details of what is right and wrong. Time and much loving care will be needed by our friends in 'incarnational intervention' to present a different view of the world, until we can trust their love, and gradually accept God as a trustworthy promise-keeping God of mercy, warmth, wisdom and love, and not feel threatened by his righteousness. Then we will find that we are more able to forgive ourselves.

There is such a thing as true guilt, of course. We are responsible for something that we have done deliberately which we should not have done. We must accept responsibility and, as far as we can, must make amends. Relief cannot come until the depth of the offence has been acknowledged, accepted and forgiven. Absolution offered before we are truly sorry can only harden our attitudes. There is then the additional guilt over accepting forgiveness that we do not deserve. A pat on the head for the child who has deliberately broken a valuable ornament and who then whimpers the well-tried formula, 'Sorry,' is not forgiveness. Forgiveness is about recognizing the wrong, but refusing to allow it to destroy the relationship. In fact this fracture can be used to deepen the relationship.

Anger

Everyone experiences anger and rage, though some feel it more violently than others. Anger feels dangerous, frightening and harmful. Nevertheless, it is an automatic and protective reaction to something which appears to be threatening our security or betraying our love. It is morally neutral. However, because it feels so explosive it is uncomfortable to live with and feels 'bad'. The issue is often complicated by the fact that we sometimes personalize anger, that is to say, we miss the basic issue and direct our feelings on to someone who seems to personify it. The patient who had a very good relationship with a doctor, for example, may resent change and so feel angry with any new doctor, blaming that person for being brusque and incompetent.

The person whose spouse has been unfaithful will usually be very angry. Love has been betrayed. But while there is anger, there is still some engagement in the relationship: the anger is an aspect of love.

The results of mishandling anger are often catastrophic and so it is understandable that many people prefer to give it a wide berth. Some people are brought up in a family where a display of anger is regarded as unacceptable. They never see it handled both openly and constructively and they are not taught how to handle it themselves. More than this, the very reaction of anger is thought to be wrong: this barrel of energy is therefore driven underground and not defused.

In one family I knew there was a code. If father raised his finger, it meant 'Be careful'; if two fingers appeared it meant 'You've already had one warning'; three fingers meant real trouble. But mother was not so straightforward: she was a patient, well-mannered woman and, for her, any big display of feeling was bad behaviour. When something displeased her she would develop the 'grey look'. Everyone knew that something was wrong, but no one knew quite what it was or who was responsible and it was not discussed. Mother's grey look had a paralyzing effect. The children would much rather have a session with father than be immobilized by mother.

The ideal, therefore, within a family, is that anger will be recognized and expressed in whatever way is appropriate. This does not always happen, as we know too well! Children must be helped to discover that when anger is expressed appropriately, it can lead to constructive change. Good relationships can still be maintained. Parents must learn to express their anger in a way that the children can tolerate and understand. And in considering all this, we must not lose sight of the fact that we all have the child and the adult within us as we experience and express our feelings.

If, as children, we are squashed down and rebuked without a fair hearing, it is unlikely we will in the future be able to handle our own or other people's anger. We may become the sort of people who cringe emotionally and constantly appease, for fear of creating or receiving damage. Or we may hold our rage down until it bursts forth in uncontrollable fury, causing an explosion that leaves everyone exhausted and confirms our own worst fears about the destructive power of anger.

So what happens? Anger that is not expressed

111

appropriately and constructively does not just evaporate. These feelings will be smothered (and often buried more deeply) in the inner person, and gradually seep into our entire personality to make us bitter and twisted, and possibly depressed. It may also leak into our bodies to help create an ulcer, arthritis, cancer or some similar condition.

The three-year-old girl I described in the previous chapter was having a very bad experience of anger. She could not carry the weight of her mother's anger, nor was it safe for her to express her own. So it was all turned into sadness and misery and directed in upon herself. Her mother strode off, putting a deliberate physical and emotional distance between herself and the child. The little one dragged after her, maintaining the wretched distance.

And so it often happens. In our anger against someone we withdraw into our internal desert island feeling sad, hurt, unloved, misunderstood, isolated and pushed-out but often not recognizing that the root of this distress is anger. Or, alternatively, we may push the offending person out of our normal life in some way.

It is hard to bear the pain of intense anger, particularly when we have to do it alone, but our very anger often makes it difficult to let anyone in on it. It is hard for the raging baby to accept love. In the midst of anger the child not only hates others but also feels unlovable. All the parents can do is to stay around calmly and not leave, however great the temptation to do so. The child will quieten eventually and then feel relieved enough to have room for the love. As we have seen, if we do not know secure love, we will either be perpetually angry with other people or we will turn the anger inside ourselves and feel guilty, bad and dangerous. Consequently, we will feel that we have to protect the object of our anger from all this awfulness: we will feel that we have to be good, helpful, kind, and caring while we smother the smouldering anger.

Another approach is that we set the person who is actually inflaming our anger on a pedestal as a way of protecting that person from it. In this way it becomes a trap. For instance, this is often seen in church congregations where the minister or vicar is revered as always right. Once church leaders are on such a pedestal, they are safe from the anger of people who do not recognize their own true feelings. People often resolutely refuse to allow the leader to get off the pedestal they have created, because the results would be too disillusioning for them.

Being unable to be angry with someone we love can indicate a fear that we may drive them away altogether, or that they may take a terrible reprisal. We are so afraid of the destructive feelings that once again we defend ourselves by protecting that person, idealizing and making excuses for them. This can happen without our being consciously aware of what we are doing. But again we are in a trap. We are afraid to test the destructive power of our feelings or the constancy of the person's love. The expression of anger would make a safer and more real relationship. A love relationship in which there is no room for anger is defective.

Similarly, anger against God is the feeling that we are ranged against an impossible 'parent' who has all the authority and power. Protest becomes useless. Only when we are free to say 'God is bad' (as the psalmist sometimes did) is there also room to say with reality that 'God is good'. It is because we have been trained to say all the time that God is good that we feel anger and resentment when God appears to let us down.

In an attempt to understand our inner needs better we could ask ourselves several questions: What are the things that make me angry? How do I express my anger? Do I know that I am angry? How do I know? What does that lead to in my personal feelings about myself or my relationships? How is the issue that provokes the anger usually resolved? This little exercise can be even more effective if it is shared with someone else and discussed with mutual honesty.

Anger is not resolved simply by letting fly at someone. We may feel better for a time if we have got it off our chest, but nothing will have been resolved just by ventilating our feelings.

The single most important way to face our anger is to have some real encounter with the other person so that some realistic negotiation at gut level is achieved. The root of the anger will be worked through and owned by both parties as a part of their total relationship. In this way, relationships are deepened and confidence is gained in dealing constructively with anger. In the future, some potentially dangerous situations can even be recognized in advance and resolved. There will be a loss of the fear of anger and increased trust in the power of love. Above all, there will be an increasing ability to make ourselves vulnerable without fear of rejection or exploitation. The child within will gain increased maturity. Those feelings that result after the engagement can be recouped into a safe home inside ourselves and channelled into a greater intimacy. We may lose a friend, sometimes, but that is the risk we take in being real.

In our negotiations we have to bear in mind that our desire to hurt someone may bear some relation to the inner hurt that we ourselves are carrying. It is important to encounter these stormy waters, difficult and dangerous though they be. The price of not doing so is heavy, in terms of the spiritual, emotional, social and physical cost. Coldness and insensitivity are not infrequently the result of some unrecognized anger and rage: so also is too much sweetness and light.

The expression of anger may also enable us to discover to what extent we are projecting our own shadow side onto someone else and hating it there. The strength of the anger could indicate the strength of this shadow projection. We certainly need to get it back into ourselves and deal with it more appropriately where it belongs. For instance, Margaret hated her husband's laid-back approach to life. She herself was always hardworking, well-organized, had everything under control and could not relax. Why did she *have* to be so uncomfortably busy? She had developed a great divide between her persona of virtue and her shadow of sluttishness. Her husband's 'laziness' could have become a repository for her shadow side. Rather than fuming at him, she might have done better to take a long, slow look at herself.

Sometimes it is not possible to tangle with the object of our anger. The person may be dead or have moved away. But even so, we can face ourselves with what we feel about the situation, ask some hard questions and discover whether or not we would feel safe and whole enough within ourselves to discuss the troublesome issues with them if this were possible. If we can reach the person in our feelings, we may be able to imagine a possible dialogue that will bring us some emotional healing and the possibility of forgiveness.

Jealousy and envy

These two emotions are both very painful to experience. Both have their roots in deep inner fear and buried anger: the sense that some loved and needed object is about to be lost; the impression that there is always some more successful rival just around the corner; the inner conviction that one is not lovable enough to hold the object of one's love, and that as soon as anyone more exciting, handsome, clever or rich appears on the horizon, the loved one will automatically be seduced away.

We are back to the old, familiar ground of the world of the child within. Some significant early experience seriously damaged our self-confidence. It could be that when as infants we were just struggling to adapt to our environment and putting out our first roots of love and trust in our parents, another baby appeared and we had to share them. The attention that we so much needed was given to someone else and we did not yet have the resources for the difficult business of sharing.

It may be that our parents did not understand this: they might have expected us to behave with a degree of adult maturity, which we did not have. Maybe for other reasons they had to give the new baby more attention than they had expected. Whatever the circumstances, we became stuck in our emotional development in this area, and ever since have been plagued with the sense of an intruder about to steal the emotional support we need. Other experiences could produce the same result. Again, rational argument does not help but personal attention, affirmation and love does. That is 'incarnational intervention'!

Love

Love is not always the easy, delightful experience that we imagine. When we love someone in a deep and personal way, we become very vulnerable. All the hidden fears, needs, and weaknesses come to the surface along with the strengths. Emotional exposure is often more difficult than physical exposure. The familiar doubts are right on the surface: Will I still be accepted if I say..? Dare I put the *whole* weight of my trust in..? The exquisite joy in discovering little by little that it *is* safe to trust more and more deeply is one of the most healing experiences that we can ever encounter. This is what love is. Conversely, the disappointment in discovering that it is not safe to trust is equally intense.

Learning to love is a slow and continuous process. Intimacy is achieved only gradually, by trial and error. The atmosphere of deep commitment makes it safe to begin to take risks and to disclose some of the deep inner feelings that are usually hidden from others' eyes and sometimes from our own. The level of communication can begin to expand and lead into deeper areas of mutual understanding. Without honest and risky communication there can be no real depth of relationship and consequently no deep love. Trust and intimacy are essential parts of love.

Where there is love there is inevitably pain as well as joy. There is the joy of being accepted, affirmed, valued and cared for as well as the joy of the physical oneness that embodies emotional oneness. There is the pain of separation, of being misunderstood at times, and the pain that comes from seeing our own shortcomings and the shortcomings of the person we love.

In love between the sexes there is immense comfort and delight to be drawn from the closeness of another person's lips, eyes, hands, arms and body. It can be so powerful and intoxicating that physical intimacy can easily be mistaken for love. There are many people who search desperately to satisfy their hunger for love through the excitement of eroticism. That is not the way. It is possible for sexual intimacy to be erotic without touching the emotional needs of the real person inside that desirable body, as many can testify with bitterness. Until those deep emotional needs are satisfied, the hungry search will continue.

The woman who likes the 'kissing and cuddling but not the rest' is a person whose basic need to be affirmed and accepted for herself has never been satisfied. The kissing and cuddling belong to her childhood needs for love, and she is really stuck there, although she submits to adult sexual activity and derives some limited pleasure from it. Her husband does not recognize this. He has his own needs. So her inner self is bypassed, and the hungry needs go unmet. Perhaps his too. It is the *relationship* that brings affirmation and joy: the physical intimacy of body is an expression of that relationship. The physical excitement cannot satisfy unless it reflects the relationship. Eroticism within the context of deep, loving, personal commitment, sensitive care and mutual understanding is a different matter entirely from eroticism that signifies hunger.

A love relationship is like a dance in which the partners keep in step, together and responsively, through the various changes of tempo. That sounds enjoyable and straightforward. It actually demands a marked degree of concentration, intelligence, awareness and sensitivity.

Self-control

So far this important ingredient in life has hardly been mentioned. What is the place of self-control? Does it have a place in healthy living or should we all express all our hurts, needs and ecstasies whenever and however we feel them?

What is self-control? It is *not* burying feelings, neither is it permanently smothering them, though it may not be convenient to express them at the exact moment when we become aware of them. We may have to struggle with our feelings, but we should aim to resolve them in a satisfactory way.

Imagine the tiny baby who is experiencing hunger, or the need to be cuddled. That child simply cannot exercise self-control. Such a concept is a nonsense and inappropriate to the child's state of maturity! The way to respond to the situation is to meet his need. The adult caregiver may find it highly inconvenient to answer the call of the baby at that moment, but the adult is in a better position to demonstrate self-control. If the baby's needs are never met satisfactorily, the child will always be whining and demanding. Self-control will be almost impossible because of the permanent emotional hunger inside.

It may be that the adult caregiver also has inner child needs that are unmet. In this case the person will have limited self-control and may respond to the incessant demands of the grizzling infant by actual physical battering. This unhappy situation is thus passed down the generations. Most parents know the impulse to batter their child but, fortunately, most are able to exercise self-control in one way or another.

However, as life goes on, most of us begin to perceive that needs will eventually be met and that promises will be kept and as a result we are increasingly able to wait. The growing ability to hold feelings in suspension is an indication of growing maturity. It is realistic to expect an older child to have a greater degree of self-control: indeed, this is a necessary part of social behaviour that must be learned. But the same conditions apply: self-control springs from the safe knowledge that basic needs will be met.

Initially, restraints are imposed upon us by our parents. As we grow we test out those restraints as our way of discovering where the boundaries lie and how far we can go with other people. It is frightening not to have any limits. As children, we may discover that kicking and screaming eventually achieve the desired result or that it can produce such unpleasant repercussions that we have to suppress our needs and let them simmer miserably and sulkily under the surface. Ideally, we learn that restraint usually has a constructive purpose: it does not mean that needs will never be met but that they will be met in the best way at the right time. In this situation we can begin to take within ourselves the restraints on our impulses and feelings. On our journey towards adulthood we can decide which of the earlier restraints we are willing to make our own and which we will reject.

As adults, the greater the degree of integration between our persona and shadow side, the greater will be our ability to control ourselves. We will be openly aware that some of our needs have been met while others have not. Self-control is not something that can be imposed satisfactorily and permanently from outside: that can come close to repression. Self-control in its truest form comes from the inside.

In one of his penetrating discourses Jesus said, 'It is what comes out of a person that makes him unclean. For from the inside, from the person's heart, come the evil ideas which lead him to do immoral things, to rob, kill, commit adultery, be greedy, and do all sorts of evil things; deceit, indecency, jealousy, slander, pride and folly — all these evil things come from inside a person and make him unclean.' These are the poisons that emerge from unmet needs, like venom from inside a snake, and to some extent we all fall into that category. But later on we read about the 'fruits' that grow out of the 'branch' which is healthily fed: 'Love, joy, peace, patience, kindness, goodness, faithfulness, humility and *self-control*.' But fruit does not appear over-night.

Without genuine ability to control ourselves, relationships can become impossible. They turn into one person manipulating the other to meet their own selfish needs. Self-control in a vacuum is not much use. Its great value is in relation to something else: the willingness to hold back or deny itself in favour of a greater good. That is maturity. We cannot deny ourselves something that we do not or could not possess;

we do not have it and so are not in a position to forgo it.

Self-control does not mean suppressing our feelings. It is knowing them and being able to express them in a way that is constructive. Self-control means knowing the strength of our feelings and how to harness them. It means being able to distinguish between our neediness and our naughtiness, and responding to each appropriately.

Self-denial and 'dying to self'

People sometimes equate the concept of self-denial with the biblical idea of 'dying to self'. Both are thought of as an injunction to obliterate our spontaneity and essential personality in order to conform to some emaciated stereotype of passivity. Or people see them as a command to push any uncomfortable feelings out of our awareness. A great sense of guilt often follows if this does not prove possible. But both these interpretations are misunderstandings of the real meaning.

True self-denial is basically a matter of self-control: knowing what would satisfy me, but being ready to put that on one side, consciously and without resentment, in order to achieve something more important. Mother Frances Dominica is a shining illustration of self-denial. She founded Helen House in Oxford, the world's first hospice for children, and she spends her life in sacrificial service of the children and their parents. Her quietly serene face tells its own story.

'Dying to self', that prickly-sounding phrase, seems to imply hair shirts, self-flagellation and other unpleasant exercises. It actually means facing and dealing with the poisonous feelings that come from within. It is not appropriate to be laden with guilt about them. It is appropriate to look at them, understand them, and call them by their name, without using any of the defence mechanisms of denial, projection and so on. The good news is that we can have God's help to do this. He offers forgiveness, hope and the possibility of change.

Feeling and knowing

There is also a time for recognizing when feelings are the channel through which destructive actions may come. An obvious example is growing physical intimacy that leads to the inevitable desire for sexual intercourse, even though one of the partners in the affair is already committed to somebody else. The *feelings* are so enticing, compelling and altogether irresistible that we can very easily be overtaken by them.

It is sometimes difficult to distinguish between love and physical desire. We can talk ourselves into believing that something we know to be dangerous and potentially hurtful for a dozen reasons is good, necessary and healthful. It is the oldest trick in the book! Whether or not you believe in the literal story of Adam and Eve in the Garden of Eden, the story of their giving in to their appetites reflects this pattern. Probably, over a period of time and with initial resistance from Eve, the desirable feelings became detached from what Eve *knew* to be right, and she went on playing with them, with disastrous consequences. It is usually true that 'the devil comes as an angel of light' and only after the deed is done does he show his self, leaving us to pick up the pieces as best we may. So what are we to do with *those* feelings?

There are certain occasions when the only healthy course is to resist them on a daily basis, to run away from them and to call on God's grace to help in time of need when our own feeble resources are not enough. God's grace comes in a surprising variety of ways to change the focus of the feelings. After that, we have to stay with the pain of 'dying to self' and allow that pain to be turned into a deep quality of awareness and quiet peace — not self-righteous virtue.

Feelings themselves do not make us into bad people. It may be that the feeling of love for someone who is not available to us, for instance, is uncomfortable and frustrating, but it is not necessarily bad. We do not have to *act* on every feeling and impulse that crosses our path. Maturity is about controlling our feelings, not about not being tempted. 'You can't stop the birds flying over your head, but you can stop them making a nest in your hair', as the old saying goes.

It is obviously important to recognize that our lives are lived within a moral context, and that there are moral guidelines within which our feelings need to be expressed. Moral rules are important for framing patterns of life which make for true human freedom and fulfilment. Moral rules themselves, however, have no power to make life good, neither can they help us to manage our feelings.

Maturity

Zoe found all this talk about being a child a bit irritating, 'How can I stop being a child?' she asked. 'When shall I become an adult? I don't want to be dependent on someone else for comfort. I want to be able to stand on my own two feet.'

She had struggled so hard against the child within. She had given it a nodding acceptance, but quickly swung back to seeing herself as a self-possessed adult. Although her rational mind could see why part of her remained childlike, her deep reaction was to despise this part. Children are weak, a nuisance, messy and in the way, she thought. She had tried to impose cerebral understandings onto her feelings; but it did not work. It never does. That is the way to repression and smothering. The leap involved in committing herself to her inner needs seemed too dangerous and frightening. She *needed* to be in control, to be competent, efficient and busy. To let go these controls felt like Humpty Dumpty falling off the wall. He would never be put together again! She could not accept that she might be put back together in a better form.

The mature person is not a person whose inner child has ceased to exist. *We all have a child within*. The mature person is someone who has found a place for the inner child and can live in peace with it, sensitively and with mutual respect.

We see that self-control bears a direct relationship to our degree of maturity. We may be adult but that does not necessarily mean that we are mature. Maturity implies a certain amount of self-understanding, integration and self-possession. This is a continuous process with no final point, in this life. How do we acquire maturity? Inevitably, life's experiences mean that we must learn something; if the experiences are, on the whole, benevolent, we shall gradually become quietly confident, able to hold the good and bad things together at the same time, to live with the joy and the sorrow, to persevere in the face of difficulty and discouragement as well as reward and encouragement and to go on building on our experience.

In addition to all this, there is that unseen and very real quality of 'grace' by which we may live: the grace God gives to us as he receives and accepts us — and as we remain attentive to the signs of his presence in our own life, not running away from his steady gaze of love. That relationship of love and trust deepens as we go along. There is no cut-off point, no time when it comes to an end. The introduction to the service of Nine Lessons and Carols from Kings College Chapel,

Cambridge, on Christmas Eve reminds us that even the death of the physical body means a continuation of that relationship 'upon another shore and in a greater light'. We shall recognize it as home when we arrive, because we have already been living in the love of Jesus Christ in this mortal life.

Suggestions for further reading

Janet Baker, *Full Circle*, Penguin Books 1984.

David Benner, *Psychotherapy and the Spiritual Quest*, Hodder and Stoughton 1989.

Jack Dominian, *The Capacity To Love*, Darton, Longman and Todd 1985.

Martin Israel, *Living Alone*, SPCK 1982.

M. Scott Peck, *The Road Less Travelled*, Touchstone 1978.

Ronald Rolheiser, *The Restless Heart*, Spire Books 1988.

John V. Taylor, *A Matter of Life and Death*, SCM Press 1986.

Also from Lion Publishing

COPING WITH DEPRESSION
Myra Chave-Jones

'Depression is as universal as the common cold.'

It may be little more than a passing mood. It may be a dark shadow, robbing life of all joy. It may make it impossible to carry out the simplest tasks. It may last for only a short time, or drag on for months and years.

What causes depression? How can we recognize it in ourselves and in others? And what help is available?

This is a helpful, practical, sympathetic book for all who suffer from depression, and for those who live close to them.

ISBN 0 85648 360 5

A selection of top titles from LION PUBLISHING

FAMILY/PRACTICAL HELP

COPING WITH DEPRESSION Myra Chave-Jones	£1.95 ☐
THE STRESS MYTH Richard Ecker	£3.95 ☐
FACE TO FACE WITH CANCER Marion Stroud	£3.95 ☐
WHEN SOMEONE YOU LOVE IS DYING Ruth Kopp	£4.95 ☐
SIMPLE SIMON Ann Lovell	£1.50 ☐
ELIZABETH JOY Caroline Philps	£1.50 ☐
THE LONG ROAD HOME Wendy Green	£1.95 ☐
YOUR MARRIAGE Peg and Lee Rankin	£2.50 ☐
GETTING MARRIED IN CHURCH Mary Batchelor	£1.95 ☐
CHARNWOOD Grace Wyatt/Clive Langmead	£2.50 ☐
SEX AND THAT Michael Lawson/Dr David Skipp	£1.75 ☐
WILL MY RABBIT GO TO HEAVEN? Jeremie Hughes	£2.95 ☐
SINGLE PARENT Maggie Durran	£1.95 ☐

All Lion paperbacks are available from your local bookshop or newsagent, or can be ordered direct from the address below. Just tick the titles you want and fill in the form.

Name (Block letters) _____

Address _____

_____

Write to Lion Publishing, Cash Sales Department, PO Box 11, Falmouth, Cornwall TR10 9EN, England.

Please enclose a cheque or postal order to the value of the cover price plus:

UK: 60p for the first book, 25p for the second book and 15p for each additional book ordered to a maximum charge of £1.90.

OVERSEAS: £1.25 for the first book, 75p for the second book, plus 28p per copy for each additional book.

BFPO: 60p for the first book, 25p for the second book, plus 15p per copy for the next seven books, thereafter 9p per book.

Lion Publishing reserves the right to show on covers and charge new retail prices which may differ from those previously advertised in the text or elsewhere, and to increase postal rates in accordance with the Post Office.